Happy Gardening.

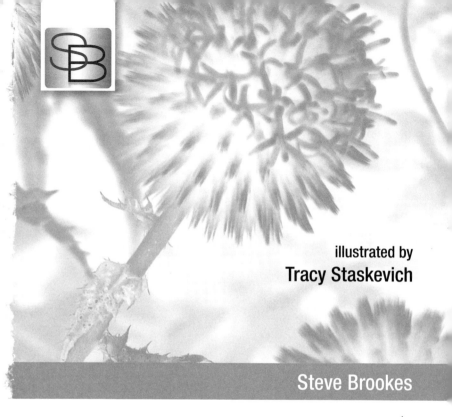

illustrated by
Tracy Staskevich

Steve Brookes

The Greatest
Gardening
Tips in the World

A 'Steve Brookes Publishing' book

www.stevebrookes.com

Illustrations:
Tracy Staskevich

Cover design:
Cliff Hayes
www.hayesdesign.co.uk

Copy editor:
Bronwyn Robertson
www.theartsva.com

Author:
Steve Brookes

First published in 2004 by Public Eye Publications

This edition published in 2010 by:
Steve Brookes Publishing, 60 Loxley Road
Stratford-upon-Avon, Warwickshire CV37 7DR
Tel: 01789 267124 / 07801 552538
Email: steve@stevebrookes.com

A CIP catalogue record for this book is available from the British Library
ISBN 978-1-905151-60-8

Printed and bound in China by Shenzhen Caimei Printing Company Ltd

To ...

... Mum
for her love and support.

... Joe, Laura & Amy
for putting up with a workaholic dad!

... My Dad,
who would have been so proud
and would have shown it to everyone!

Contents

A few words from Steve …

I began writing this book over 30 years ago at the very frost tender age of … well let's just say I was in short trousers with a great love of plants and nature! I began collecting gardening tips then and writing them down in old school exercise books, intending, one day, to publish them as a great horticultural work. Some tips were imparted to me by my grandfather and other wise old 'sages' of the gardening world, whose paths crossed mine on my green and pleasant journey through adolescence.

The dramatic streak within me resulted in the offer of a trial with the prestigious Royal Shakespeare Company when I was 15, but I was undeterred and resolved to pursue a career in horticulture and tread the soil rather than the boards. My enthusiasm for gardening was fuelled in my late teens by a wonderful TV gardener with a soft Yorkshire accent and a passion for plants that captivated me – Geoffrey Smith. I knew then that gardening was to be my vocation. As my career grew, so did the number of amazing tips I had collected. Eventually I decided to test the tips to see how many really did work and work out why. A few years spent as a soil scientist certainly helped in this regard.

Those tips that did work (and there were many!) are included, at last, in this book. Some of the tips are common sense, some are amusing, and others seem, well, just so wacky that they couldn't possibly work, but they all do.

With some, I have tried to explain in more detail exactly how and why they work. If you need further convincing – just try them! I must also point out that it was a twang of nostalgia that led me to stick with putting the old imperial measurements first in the text. Those who remember times when a foot was 12 inches and a meter was something the gasman called to read will know just where I'm coming from.

I really hope that you find using the tips, advice and plant lists as interesting and rewarding as it has been for me collecting them. Space has not allowed me to elaborate on the plants in the lists but you should find researching them further an exciting task in itself. The tips have been shown to work on many occasions but there can be no guarantee that they will work every time as all gardens and conditions can vary. They are, however, fun, rewarding, money saving, and environmentally friendly and are considered by me to be 'The Greatest Gardening Tips in the World'. I have left a few pages free for you to jot down any useful tips that you find on your travels. If you find any really amazing ones – let me know.

Happy gardening!

Steve.

Of all the
wonderful things in
the wonderful universe,
nothing seems to me
more surprising than
the planting of a seed
in the blank earth and
the result thereof.

Julie Moir Messervy

Germination, planting & cultivation

chapter 1
Germination, planting & cultivation

Why pick a whole cucumber when half will do?

How many times have you picked a whole cucumber from the greenhouse and had to throw half of it away a week or so later when it has gone soft? Next time remember this and just cut half a cucumber, or however much you need from the fruit on the plant. Leave the remainder still attached and cover the end with cling film held in place with a rubber band. It will stay fresh on the plant a lot longer than in the fridge.

Containerised carrots

Freshly pulled carrots can be enjoyed throughout the year, even on Christmas Day. Choose a short rooted variety and sow thinly, about ¼" (6mm) deep, in used 4 litre ice cream containers filled with free draining compost. Ensure that the container has drainage holes in the bottom and keep in a well-lit, cool, spare room or frost-free greenhouse. OK, you won't get a vast quantity of carrots this way but you have the thrill of an out of season crop. A good variety to try this novel growing idea with is 'Pamex', the perfectly round baby carrot. For something really unusual and fun, grow 'Purple Haze F1' – a purple carrot that is really sweet and can be pulled when very small.

Cotton on to these free ties

Next time you are walking past a skip have a peek inside and see if anyone has discarded an old cotton mop head. If so you will have got yourself literally hundreds of free plant ties, each about 14" (35cm) long and useful for many tying jobs around the garden. Soak the mop head in a weak bleach solution first to sterilise it, wash in detergent then rinse, dry and get pulling!

A sandy bottom for your bulbs

The performance of your spring flowering bulbs in their first, and future years, can often be dictated at planting time. Wrong planting depth, poor drainage and air gaps beneath the bulb are the most important problems to avoid. With planting depth, too deep can result in a 'blind' bulb – one that produces leaf growth but no flower – and too shallow can provide easy pickings for the hungry squirrel! A good rule of thumb is to make the hole twice the depth of the bulb you are planting.

Both drainage and air gap problems can be sorted out with nothing more than a small handful of sharp sand placed in the hole when you plant the bulbs. Pressed gently into the sand, the bulb will be able to cope much better with any excess water in the soil without going rotten. Air gaps beneath a bulb can often occur when you use a pointed trowel to make the planting hole. The round-bottom bulb then sits in the hole but not always onto soil. The new roots will then have difficulty in anchoring the bulb effectively and taking up water and nutrients. The small amount of sand added to the hole will ensure even contact for the bottom of the bulb and will allow the roots to grow without a struggle.

Nature's lunchbox

I'm always keen to make explanations as easy as possible to understand, and when it comes to explaining bulbs there is a simple analogy. Think of bulbs as just lunchboxes full of food. A bulb spends the months after flowering packing itself with food. From the time a bulb begins to shoot again in winter it is only using food that it stored during the previous spring and summer.

Feeding bulbs when they are shooting and before they flower will only result in excess leaf growth and poor flowering. As soon as the flowering is over that is the time to feed the bulbs well with foliar and a granular feed. Never remove any of the foliage until it is completely brown and pulls away easily. All of the goodness from these dying bits of foliage is valuable food which will be stored back in the lunchbox for a blooming good show next spring.

Immovable orchids

There are more species of orchid than any other plant in the world. The huge orchid family contains 25,000 species and over 100,000 hybrids in 835 genera (orchid plant groups). They also have some of the most intricate and beautiful flower structures on earth.

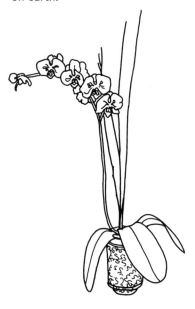

If you want longer lasting orchid flowers then it is vital not to move the plant at all when it is in flower. Even a slight turn of the pot can cause the flower stalks to twist and the blooms to drop off. Left alone an orchid can hold its flowers for months. Remember also that most orchids that you will buy from garden centres and supermarkets for home enjoyment come from a tropical rainforest habitat. Try to mimic their natural conditions by giving them a position with dappled sunlight with plenty of humidity. Never water them with ordinary tap water which can contain too much lime. Instead use cooled boiled tap water or preferably rainwater than has been allowed to reach room temperature first.

> The cure for this ill,
> is not to sit still,
> Or frowst with
> a book by the fire;
> But to take a large
> hoe and a shovel also,
> And dig till you
> gently perspire.

Rudyard Kipling

Steve's recipe for a perfect wildlife tapestry hedge

This mixed hedge is a wonderful way of creating a wildlife paradise, even in a small garden. It is easily managed and can be kept as low as 3' (90cm) if required. It will give all year round interest and colour for you and the wildlife in your garden and the use of species plants with colourful leaves, protective thorns, different flowers & berries and autumn nuts creates an ever-changing, delightful hedge.

The whole hedge is bound together with two different ivies giving a beautiful tapestry effect. Trimmed once a year in late winter, before the birds start nesting, this hedge will give you, and nature, years of pleasure. The recipe itself is mouth-watering and the result should be breathtaking!

- *Crataegus monogyna* (Common hawthorn)
- *Corylus avellana* (Common hazel)
- *Fagus sylvatica* (Common beech)
- *Fagus sylvatica 'Pupurea'* (Copper beech)
- *Cornus sanguinea* OR *Cornus mas* (Flowering dogwood)
- *Ilex aquifolium 'Argentea marginata'* (Female holly)
- *Ilex aquifolium 'Atlas'* (Male holly)
- *Prunus spinosa 'Pupurea'* (Blackthorn)
- *Rosa rugosa 'Alba'* (White hedging rose)
- *Rosa rugosa ''Scabrosa''* (Deep pink hedging rose)
- *Hedera helix* (Common ivy – get two vigorous varieties, one plain and one variegated)

Hey man, cool grass!

You might have noticed how reluctant grass seed is to germinate in the warmth of summer but seems to do it much faster in spring and autumn? This is no reflection on the quality of the seed or your expert preparation of the area to be seeded; it's all to do with a peculiar fact about grass seed. It germinates, not because of the actual temperature but due to a sudden change in temperature – the sort of condition that you find more readily in spring and autumn. Summer sown grass seed can be tricked into germinating quickly by keeping it in the freezer for a couple of days prior to planting. The sudden change in temperature from the cold freezer to the warm soil at sowing time is all that is required to ensure speedy germination.

Shower caps are the tops

When staying in quality hotels how many people think to take the shower caps away with them? Not many. In fact remove it from the bathroom each day and room service will leave you a new one. Collect as many as you can because these elasticated plastic caps make ideal propagator tops for large flowerpots or even half seed trays. They are easy to take on and off and do away with the need to find a plastic bag and an elastic band.

Remember, though, to remove the shower cap regularly and shake off any condensation. If the water droplets are allowed to fall onto the leaves of seedlings they could magnify the sun's rays and burn holes in the young plants.

Aspirin – just what the plant doctor ordered

Do you have a plant suffering from stunted growth? Does the label say 8' but you've only got 8"? Your plant has probably run short of growth hormone and has lost the ability to make any more. You won't find plant growth hormone at your local garden centre and, even if you could, it would be pretty expensive.

Never fear because, without realising it, your own medicine cabinet might have some. It will not be labelled 'plant growth hormone' but labelled 'soluble aspirin'. This is made from salicylic acid – almost identical to the naturally occurring growth hormone in plants and would you believe it, they can't tell the difference. One soluble aspirin in a pint of water every couple of weeks will kick the plant back into growth and it can start making more hormone for itself. As soon as you see new growth appear you can stop the aspirin treatment.

Cute cane top covers

The garden can be a dangerous place for your eyes if you have short bamboo canes around supporting your plants. There are many things that you can put on top of a cane to make it safer but I think one of the best is a rubber baby's bottle teat. If you haven't got a relation with a new baby make friends with someone who does have a new addition to the family and scrounge their old teats – they fit perfectly onto a cane and could just save your eyesight one day.

Longer-lasting labels

Even if you use a permanent marker pen on your plant labels, the ink will still eventually fade to nothing in the sunlight.

To stop this happening, as soon as you have written on the label, give the writing a quick covering of clear nail polish. The ink will be fixed by the polish and will never fade. This also means that you don't have to hunt for a waterproof marker – any one will do.

An added benefit is that, at the end of the season, when you need to clean off the labels for re-use next year all you need to do is lift the edge of the nail polish layer with a sharp knife and peel off. Magically the polish will take with it every bit of the marker pen ink, leaving you a perfectly clean label.

Protection for old tools

I think you will agree that old gardening tools, passed down from generation to generation give both nostalgic connotations of bygone gardening days as well as a lovely feel in the hands. Sadly these old tools won't have the benefit of stainless steel manufacturing and can become rusted if not cleaned thoroughly after each use. The solution, according to my friend and mentor Geoffrey Smith, is to make up a 'pontica' bucket – a bucket filled with sharp sand soaked with old engine oil. After use, the trusty old spade, fork or trowel is plunged vigorously up and down into the sand. Any remains of soil are removed by the sand and the tool is left with a thin coating of rust preventing oil. Magic!

" The gardening season officially begins on January 1st and ends on December 31st. "

Anon

BIG SCOOP SAVES TIME & MESS

Using a trowel to get compost out of one of the large bags can be a frustrating experience! Just as you reach the lip of the bag it bends in and knocks most of the compost off the trowel. You can avoid this by making your own compost scoop very simply from one of the 2 litre plastic pop bottles with the built-in handle. Cut the bottle at an angle about 8" (20cm) along from the cap end, making sure that the handle is in line with the angled cut. This scoop will hold about three times the amount of a trowel so will save you time as well as your sanity. As long as you have remembered to screw the top back on of course!

Drainpipe supports

Certain plants such as runner beans, clematis and sweet peas, benefit from support from the time they are planted. Tying them to canes can be fiddly and cause damage to the thin stems. A really good alternative is to use a section of small diameter plastic drainpipe cut to a length about 2" (5cm) higher than the plant. Slide the pipe gently over the plant and push about 2" (5cm) into the soil. Not only will this provide support but will also prevent wind damage to the tender plant AND will deter those pesky slugs and snails. Good eh?

Stylish hanging baskets

Next time you clear out your wardrobe, keep any dark coloured woolly jumpers or fleeces you intend to throw out as they make great linings for hanging baskets. You can easily cut out planting holes and they are big enough to fit any size of basket. Dark colours are better as they look less obvious when wet and absorb the heat to give your baskets more protection on cooler evenings.

Hoe, hoe, hoe!

One of the most underrated and underused tools in the garden is the trusty old hoe. Hours of back breaking weeding can be avoided if you just spend a few minutes with a Dutch or flat hoe each week. Newly emerging weed seedlings have their lives cut short if you just hoe the top ½″ (12mm) of soil. This is best done in the sunshine so any seedlings that do avoid the fatal chop will wither and die quickly on the soil surface. Getting the hoe out early like this stops the weeds from producing seed, which, given the chance, they will do before you know it. In fact some weeds can actually shorten their life-cycles to benefit from more favourable conditions.

Recycled rolls

Seeds of plants which have a long tap root, such as sweet peas and parsley, do really well when sown in the cardboard tubes from the middle of toilet rolls. The whole tubes can then be planted out at the appropriate time without disturbing the roots of the plants.

Hot coldframe

If you have tender plants that need over-wintering but you don't have a greenhouse then worry not, just invest in a relatively inexpensive coldframe. Fill a number of sacks with grass cuttings and damp them down well. Put your plants into the coldframe and surround them with the filled sacks. The rotting grass will generate enough heat during the winter to keep the plants warm and healthy until spring. If the weather is forecast to be particularly cold then lay some extra sacks on top of the coldframe for added insulation.

All dressed up

Never underestimate the importance of top dressing your permanent container plantings. Herbaceous perennials, bulbs and shrubs growing in containers can benefit immensely from the removal of the top 2" (5cm) of compost every spring and replacing it with fresh John Innes No 3 compost (or ericaceous compost if appropriate). Doing this will dispose of any slug, snail or other pest eggs and weed seeds that reside in this top layer, as well as providing a more friable surface ready to receive water and liquid feed. I mention John Innes No 3 compost as this is a far better medium for perennial plants in containers. Being a soil-based compost, it provides better drainage than peat-based ones and doesn't shrink in volume as the latter often do after a year or so.

Steve's top summer stunners

Some plants just have a 'wow' factor in the summer garden. A comprehensive list would go on and on. It was difficult – but here are my favourites …

- *Allium flavum, Allium* 'Globemaster' and *Allium karataviense* (Ornamental onions)
- *Anemone rivularus* (Windflower)
- *Catananche caerulea* (Cupid's dart)
- *Clematis* 'Bees' Jubilee'
- *Clematis* 'The President'
- *Eremurus x isabellinus* 'Cleopatra' (Foxtail lily)
- *Eryngium x zabelii, Eryngium variifolium* and *Eryngium alpinum* (Sea holly)
- *Euphorbia griffithii* 'Dixter' (Spurge)
- *Lavendua stoechas* (French lavender)
- *Lobelia* 'Bee's Flame'
- *Lonicera x tellmanniana* (Honeysuckle)
- *Papaver rhoeas* 'Mother of Pearl' (Poppy)
- *Passiflora caerulea* (Passion flower)
- *Penstemon* 'Stapleford Blue'
- *Philadelphus* 'Belle Etoile' (Mock orange)
- *Phlox paniculata* 'Barnwell'
- *Rosa* 'Louise Odier' (Bourbon rose)
- *Rosa* 'Souvenir du Docteur Jamain'
- *Scabiosa caucasica* 'Clive Greaves' (Scabious)
- *Sidalcea* 'Elsie Heugh' (False mallow)

Space saving cuttings

Here is a great way of taking numerous cuttings without utilising any bench space at all. Firstly you will need to fix a string line, at head height, across the greenhouse, potting shed, conservatory or anywhere that is brightly lit but can be protected from full sun. Take your cuttings in the usual way, cutting at an angle just below a leaf joint, making the piece of stem about 4"–5" (10cm – 12.5cm) long and use hormone rooting powder if necessary. Next push the cutting into the corner of a clear plastic freezer bag containing about 2" (5cm) deep of well-moistened, good quality multi-purpose compost mixed with a little sharp sand for extra drainage. Loosely gather the bag opening and with a clothes peg, hang to a previously fixed string line. There should be no need to add further water to the bag because what is there will condense back into the compost and, providing you have gathered the neck of the bag loosely, fresh air can still reach the cutting.

You will easily see those cuttings that have taken as they will eventually produce white roots at the side of the compost in the bag. These then be carefully removed, transplanted into 3" (7.5cm) pots and given valuable space on the windowsill or greenhouse staging. Those that don't root can be discarded with nothing lost apart from a bit of compost. You can even turn the plastic bags inside out, wash and re-use. Avoid re-using the compost though as it may contain mold spores from a rotted cutting. Taking cuttings in this way means that you can really experiment and try all sorts of plants without worrying about space.

The perfect start for tiny seeds

Sowing very tiny seeds thinly can be a difficult task. If we are talking about begonia seeds you also need to be able to see them first! Effective spacing of small seeds can be easily achieved with nothing more than an empty toothpaste tube and a packet of non-fungicidal wallpaper paste. First cut the bottom off the toothpaste tube and clean out well with warm water. Next, in a small bowl and depending on how many seeds you have to sow, mix two or three tablespoons of the wallpaper paste to a very thin gel with tepid water. Sprinkle your tiny seeds into the gel and mix very quickly with a table fork.

Amazingly, the wonder of physics takes place and spaces the seeds like atoms, equidistant to each other in the gel. Using a fork also ensures that air is incorporated into the gel. Now carefully transfer the mix into the toothpaste tube using a teaspoon. Take your prepared seed tray of compost and roll down the tube from the bottom, whilst squeezing the gel into a drill in the surface – just like using an icing bag. Finally cover the gel if necessary, with a thin layer of compost or vermiculite. Some seeds will not need covering as they need light to germinate but the instructions on the packet will help you. Your seeds are now not only evenly spread but also have a water reservoir in the gel, air and some extra food when the cellulose of the wallpaper paste eventually breaks down. They will quickly germinate and have a brilliant start in life.

Sugar keeps your Christmas tree sweet

A Christmas tree devoid of needles can be a common sight in our modern, centrally-heated rooms. The dry air causes the needles to drop despite your best efforts of keeping it standing in water. You can buy sprays for the leaves, which are reputed to help, but a good way of reducing needle drop is to keep your water reservoir topped up with sugar water. A 1lb (½ kg) bag of sugar dissolved in 2 gallons (9 litres) of water will do the trick. Use this solution every time the water reservoir needs topping up. The sugar is taken into the plant system and helps to keep the needles attached.

Growing your own mini-turves

When you have small dead patches of grass to repair on your lawn the easiest solution is to grow your own mini-turves. Line a half or full sized seed tray with about 6 layers of absorbent kitchen towel and moisten well. Sow your grass seed thickly over the surface and press the seed into the wet towel. Place the trays on a well-lit windowsill, keep moist and turn regularly. After a couple of weeks you will have a mini-turf growing through the kitchen towel. When the grass is about ½" (12mm) high you can lift out your 'turf', cut to size with scissors and set in the prepared spot on the lawn. Growing it in this way you have avoided loss of seedlings to the birds, established a good root system and provided a moisture retentive medium for the first few months. And you feel a very clever gardener!

Bottomless pots for top tomatoes

Growing tomatoes in a grow bag is certainly a space saving way but you can increase yield and make staking, watering and feeding easier with a simple adaptation at planting time. Instead of planting the tomato plants directly into the grow bag, plant them into 7" (18cm) diameter bottomless plastic flowerpots pushed about 2" (5cm) deep into the revealed compost of the grow bag. The plants get established quicker in the added depth of compost before competing with the roots of the other plants in the main part of the grow bag. Watering can be undertaken with less wasteful run-off and the feeding of each plant is more controllable.

Fast food germination

If you want to germinate small quantities of seeds and don't want the windowsill cluttered with seed trays then, instead, use the polystyrene hinged burger boxes from the fast food joints – they are perfect. All you need to do is to make some holes in the base with a hot knitting needle for drainage. The polystyrene gives great insulation and germination is speeded up. Be sure to leave the lid open as soon as the seedlings appear. Drip trays for your 'mini-propagators' can be easily made by cutting another burger box in half.

Another, simple alternative is to use empty, washed butter or margarine containers. Most even come complete with an indented lid which serves as the perfect drip tray.

The pop bottle mini cloche

Always have a supply of homemade individual cloches handy for those late frost emergencies. To make them, simply save empty, clear plastic pop bottles of various sizes and cut off the bottoms. Place over the small, tender plants and push a little way into the soil. Remember to screw the lid on at night but remove it during the day.

The houseplant pick-me-up

Many plants in containers, particularly houseplants, can suffer from magnesium deficiency – recognisable by a browning of the leaves between the veins. Trace element feeds can rectify the problem but once again you could probably have saved money by first taking a look in your bathroom cabinet. What you need to find is some Epsom salts (magnesium sulphate). This is the perfect way to revitalise those plants that are short of magnesium. One teaspoon of the salts to a pint of water every couple of weeks and the plant is back on its feet. It really is the perfect pick-me-up.

Quick tip

FREE TOMATO PLANTS

When removing the first few side shoots from your tomato plants, don't throw them all in the compost bin. Instead, plant up some of them in 3" (7.5cm) pots. They will easily root giving you plants to fill in any gaps and produce later fruits when the glut of summer fruit is over.

The African violet experience

Sometimes plants really amaze you with their requirements
for success. African violets are one such plant and actually
thrive in a situation where most other plants wouldn't last
five minutes – by the glass on a cold north-facing windowsill.
They hate being wet and don't like sunlight much either so
only water them when the leaves begin to wilt (yes – that dry!).
Given these conditions they will flourish and flower for
much longer.

If you have ever grown one then you will know that the flower
colour can be wonderful. To make the bloom colours almost
fluorescent water the plant with the tepid water in which you
have just boiled eggs. African violets have the uncanny ability
to utilise extra calcium to give this amazing flower colour
effect. Enough calcium leaches out of the eggshells when you
boil them to make the water a perfect source for the plant.

Easy cuttings with oasis

Taking cuttings can be a tricky business with a tendency for the plant material to get over watered and go rotten before it has had a chance to make roots. Then there is the trauma of transplanting which can cause major root disturbance. Both these challenges can easily be met by inserting the cutting into an inch square cube of wet flower arranger's oasis. Keep the block moist and plant the whole thing carefully into a pot at the first sign of roots showing through the sides.

This is especially effective for fuchsia cuttings, with which many people seem to struggle. You would think that wet oasis would hold too much water around the bottom of the cutting stem. In fact the opposite is true. Water is held in the tiny, absorbent grains of the oasis material and is only taken out by the new cutting roots as they appear. Enough water vapour exists in the minute air spaces to ensure the cutting doesn't dry out.

Split personality

After three years or so that big hosta with the big personality can begin to show its age and not look so stately. This is the time to split it (in the spring), replant the best bits and give the rest away to deserving friends. Splitting the plants is easy. Just dig the whole clump up and insert two garden forks, back to back, between the shoots. Push the fork handles apart and the roots shoot disentangle. Repeat this as necessary to get 6" (15cm) diameter clumps.

Steve's choice of formal & informal hedging plants

Hedges can often add wonderful structure and definition to a garden where a wall or fence would look too austere and lifeless. They are also a boon for wildlife that might otherwise struggle to find sanctuary. Formal or informal? It's up to you, so here are my choices …

FORMAL:

- *Buxus sempervirens* (Box)
- *Carpinus betulus* (Common hornbeam)
- *Fagus sylvatica* (Common beech)
- *Ilex aquifolium* (Holly)
- *Ligustrun ovalifolium* (Oval leaf privet)
- *Prunus laurocerasus* (Cherry laurel)
- *Prunus lusitanica* (Portugal laurel)
- *Taxus baccata* (Yew)
- *Thuja plicata* (Western red cedar)

INFORMAL:

- *Acer campestre* (Field maple)
- *Berberis darwinii* (Barberry)
- *Berberis stenophylla* (Barberry)
- *Chaenomeles speciosa* (Ornamental quince)
- *Cotoneaster simonsii*
- *Escallonia rubra var. macrantha*
- *Elaeagnus macrophylla*
- *Euonymus japonicus*
- *Forsythia* species
- *Photinia fraseri* 'Red Robin'
- *Pyracantha* species (Firethorn)
- *Rosa rugosa* (Hedgehog rose)
- *Rosa* 'Felicia'
- *Spirea billardii* 'Triumphans'
- *Viburnum tinus*

True recycling

Without doubt the best universal plant ties, especially for roses, are thin strips of cycle inner tube. There is nothing better. Apart from being almost impossible to break, they stretch a bit to allow for movement of the plant in windy conditions and they are free. If rose thorns do penetrate the rubber, it will not tear so the tie keeps on working. Local cycle repair shops are throwing out old inner tubes by the dozen and should be more than happy to give you a few. They might also give you a strange look but just smile sweetly and keep then guessing. Cut the rubber into various lengths and widths for a multitude of garden uses. What a great, useful way to spend a cold winter's evening – with a bottle of red wine and half a dozen inner tubes. Who says romance is dead?

Your cuttings kit

Don't get the wrong idea with this tip. You have to ask permission first. Whenever you are out visiting friends' gardens or on a country walk always have a 'cuttings kit' in your pocket. This indispensable item consists of two or three small plastic sandwich bags, a few short lengths of garden twine or elastic bands, a few sheets of very damp kitchen towel and a small sharp penknife. Armed thus you will always be prepared should you spot a 'must-have' cutting or two. Wrap the end of the cutting in a sheet of damp tissue, pop into a plastic bag, tie the top and the plant material should survive until you get back home where you can properly, and deal with the planting of your new freebie.

Paraffin protection

Mice, you will find, are particularly fond of newly planted pea and bean seeds. Mice on the other hand are not exactly turned on by the smell of paraffin. In fact they hate it. The solution? Simply soak your pea and bean seeds in paraffin for half an hour before sowing. The seed coat absorbs enough paraffin to keep the rodents away until the seeds have safely germinated and has no detrimental effect on the plants. If you find mice are also pinching your spring flowering bulbs then soak the bulbs in a solution of 1 tablespoon of paraffin to 1 pint of water for an hour before planting. This should keep your bulbs safe from rodent theft.

Seal shrubs before summer moving

Moving shrubs in the middle of summer can be a dangerous thing. Often, until they become re-established, they will lose more water through their leaves than they can replace from the soil, and the resultant dying plant is an all too common sight. If you really do have to move a shrub at this difficult time of year or indeed any time when the weather is a bit warm and dry, protection from desiccation can easily be achieved. Simply spray the whole plant an hour or so before lifting with a weak solution of non-fungicidal cellulose wallpaper paste, ensuring that both sides of the leaves are covered. The paste will dry and seal the leaves thus preventing any water loss. The plant can then be moved to its new home and allowed to settle in and recover for a few days before the paste is gently hosed off the leaves.

"A man should never plant a garden larger a garden larger than his wife can take care of.

Anon

Super sealant support

The preparation required to clothe a wall or fence with climbing plants can be quite involved and time consuming. There will be hooks or nails to screw or hammer in followed by an ugly

lattice work of twine or wire to attach so that the plants can be tied in as they grow and spread out. The problem is that the plants have minds of their own and hence never seem to grow in the direction you expect.

Then there is the problem, a year or so down the line, of having to re-point the wall or apply a preservative treatment to the fence on which the plants are growing. Everything has to be untied, unwound and then reattached later – often at the expense of some delicate young shoots that were growing happily before.

There is an easier way. Climbing plants such as clematis, honeysuckle and jasmine can be firmly held to a wall or fence by simply using clear silicone sealant bought from the DIY store. Decide where you want the stem of the plant to go and put a 1" (2.5cm) diameter blob of sealant at the appropriate place on the wall or fence. Allow about 10 minutes for setting then gently push the stem of the climber right into the middle of the blob of sealant. The climber will be held firmly against the support and the sealant will stretch to cope with the expanding stem. As the plant grows just keep adding more blobs of sealant which will be neatly hidden by the foliage of the plant. If you ever need to reposition the climber or temporarily remove it for painting or repairs then simply prize off the sealant and carefully cut it off the plant stem. When you are ready just reaffix with new sealant, maybe taking the plants in a different direction this time – it's up to you. This natty method of plant support does away with the bother of nails, hooks, wires etc … and is almost invisible.

Egg box seed collector

Often we become so wrapped up in buying seeds and plants to grow in our gardens we forget that, every late summer and autumn, nature has a 'plant one get thousands for free' offer. I'm talking about the countless free seeds available from trees, shrubs and spent perennials around the garden, so don't be too keen to tidy up the borders until you have availed yourself of all the freebies.

An empty egg box makes an ideal collecting container for these many sorts of free seeds. Carefully tap the dead flowered stems into the egg box compartments, labelling each one accordingly with a marker pen. Back inside the house, carefully make a hole one at a time in the bottom of each egg box compartment and let the seeds fall out into individual paper envelopes marked with the details of the plant and date of collection. The small wage envelopes from a stationers are ideal for this. Store the envelopes in a used ice cream or similar container in the fridge or freezer until sowing time the following spring.

Spray protection

If you really have to resort to chemical spraying for difficult weeds such as bindweed, mare's-tail and ground elder, then look to protect the surrounding plants from any spray drift, even on a still day. Different sized bottomless plastic bottles are good for small plant protection, with buckets and even plastic dustbins for the larger specimens. With systemic weed killers it only takes a little of the solution touching the leaves of a prize plant to cause heartbreaking results so don't take any chances.

RED CARPET FOR YOUR BEANS

You can help prevent the flowers on runner and French beans falling before they have set by ensuring that the plants never run short of water during the growing period. Even a short period of drought early in the plants' lives can effect the production of beans later on. To keep the soil from drying out a good tip is to lay strips of old carpet around the plants, or even lay the carpet down first and cut holes for planting or sowing. This carpet 'mulch' will also warm the soil for faster germination of seeds and growth of the plants.

Hot bath before planting

Autumn is a good time to be planting new shrubs or moving existing ones around the garden because the root systems have a chance to develop before the plant comes back into full growth in spring. However, even autumn days can get really chilly and the soil temperature can drop considerably. To avoid the plant suffering a check to growth if the soil is chilled, soak the new planting hole with boiling water half an hour before planting – it makes all the difference.

Having been berated by an elderly lady gardener on the possible boiling of earthworms when using this tip, I now add the extra advice that you should leave the dug hole open for half an hour before pouring in the water so that the worms have buried themselves deeper in the soil. Personally I would rather have a few dead worms than a dead plant!

Borrow some pollen for a feast of fruit

Not everyone has room for more than a couple of small fruit trees in their garden, and choosing them can be a headache because many varieties need the presence of another suitable pollinating fruit tree of the same species in the vicinity.

A neat way of getting round this problem is to find another garden in your area with the pollinating tree you require (nurseries will give you a list of suitable trees) and beg a sprig or two of flowering growth in spring. Put the ends of these pieces into a cut off plastic pop bottle of water and hang in your fruit tree. Amazingly the insects will pollinate your fruit flowers using the pollen from the borrowed flowering stems!

Cutting remarks

If you find it difficult to get cuttings of particular plants to root, then use a much simpler approach. Take a couple of cuttings from these plants every month from spring until late autumn. The plant won't mind and you are sure to have success on some occasions. Also don't be too heavy handed with the hormone rooting powder! As a rule of thumb, if you can easily see the powder on the end of the cutting you have used too much. A tiny speck is all that is needed to trick the end of the stem into producing roots. Finally, never use the rooting powder on pelargonium or other fleshy plant cuttings. These will root quite happily without help and the powder can actually have a detrimental effect by clogging up the stem and cause it to rot.

Steve's choice plants for a pond

Ponds make superb focal points in the garden. They extend the range of plants that can be grown and bring wildlife into the area. The following plants are a good selection for any pond ...

- *Aponogeton distachyos* (Water hawthorn)
- *Azolla caroliniana* (Fairy moss – requires winter protection)
- *Butomus umbellatus* (Flowering rush)
- *Calla palustris* (Bog arum)
- *Calthea palustris* (Marsh marigold)
- *Elodea crispa* (Oxygenating plant)
- *Hottonia palustris* (Water violet)
- *Iris pseudacorus* (Yellow flag iris)
- *Marsilea quadrifolia* (Water clover)
- *Mimulus luteus* (Monkey flower)
- *Myriophyllum aquaticum* (Parrot's feather – oxygenating plant)
- *Persicaria amphibia* (Amphibious bistort)
- *Ranunculus aquatilis* (Water crow-foot)
- *Stratiodes aloides* (Water soldier)
- *Typha latifolia variegata* (Variegated bulrush)
- *Typha latifolia* (Reedmace)
- *Typha minima* (Dwarf bulrush – for the smaller pond)
- *Veronica beccabunga* (Water pimpernel)

Bed & breakfast for the butterflies

Stinging nettles and thistles may not be the first plants on your list for a beautiful garden but they should be if you want to encourage butterflies and other beneficial insects to assist in the pollination of your plants. Pollination gives you free seeds from the flower bed and plentiful crops of beans, cucumbers, tomatoes etc ... on the vegetable plot. Butterflies will not feed on the same plants as they breed on, so as well as having lots of buddleias, scabious, sedums and other butterfly feeding stations, make sure you provide them with a breeding bed or they will go elsewhere to lay their eggs. Stinging nettles and thistles offer the butterflies protection for their newly emerged caterpillars, so keep a small, managed patch of these plants in the bottom corner of the garden.

Ring the changes in your flower border

If you can discover them at boot fairs and junkyards, try to get hold of some of the metal bands from around wooden beer barrels or wine casks. You can often find different sizes and they make attractive circular planting areas for bulbs and sowings of annual flower seeds. Place the rings on the soil surface in your chosen pattern and plant or sow into them as you would normally do. When the bulbs or seedlings start to appear you can remove the metal rings and store for use the following year.

Steve's top must-have wildlife attracting plants

If, like me, you are a wildlife-loving gardener then you will definitely want some (or all!) of these plants in your garden ...

- *Allium hollandicum* 'Purple Sensation' (Ornamental onion)
- *Amelanchier lamarckii* (Snowy mespilus)
- *Aster novae-angelica* (Michaelmas daisy)
- *Berberis darwinii* (Barberry)
- *Buddleia davidii* (Butterfly bush)
- *Caryopteris clandonensis*
- *Cotoneaster* 'Coral Beauty'
- *Digitalis species* (Foxgloves)
- *Echinops species* (Globe thistle)
- *Eryngium species* (Sea holly)
- *Lavender angustifolia* 'Hidcote' (English lavender)
- *Lavender stoechas* (French lavender)
- *Malus* 'Red Jade' (Weeping crab)
- *Marjoram* (Oregano)
- *Nepeta sibirica* (Catmint)
- *Philadelphus* 'Beauclerk' (Mock orange)
- *Rosa* (single) species (Dog rose)
- *Salvia officinalis* (Sage)
- *Santolina chamaecyparissus* 'Small Ness' (Cotton lavender)
- *Scabiosa species* (Scabious)
- *Sedum spectabile* (Ice plant)

For ripe tomatoes – go bananas!

Towards the end of the growing season, tomatoes both inside and out, become very slow to ripen. This is due to a reduction in the intensity or lux of the sunlight, which needs to be high to trigger the production of the gas, ethylene, in the tomato skins to ripen them (all very technical this isn't it?!). What you need to know is how to ripen the green tomatoes. The answer is simple – a pound of bananas! Hang the bananas individually amongst the tomato plants. The bananas' skins give off loads of ethylene as they quickly ripen and before you know it any reluctant green tomatoes will have gone red.

Be prepared for new arrivals

You never know when you will need to plant up a cutting. It might be one that you have been given by a generous gardening friend or perhaps you have brought some back from a visit to another garden (with permission of course!). It is a good idea to always have a tray of prepared cutting compost ready in the shed or greenhouse so you can pot up that potential new plant without a delay which could be make the difference between success and failure. A mix of two parts ordinary multi-purpose compost to one part sharp sand and one part horticultural grit is ideal as it gives the excellent drainage required for rooting. When the plant is growing strongly it can be moved to a the appropriate compost-rich medium.

POT LININGS

Large terracotta pots always look wonderful on the patio but, because of the porous nature of clay, the compost in them tends to dry out quickly. Avoid this problem at planting time, by lining the sides of the pots with plastic carrier bags, making sure that they are hidden under the top surface of the compost. Water loss from the pot is then considerably reduced.

Keep those secateurs handy

Never go into the garden without a pair of secateurs in your hand. Nine times out of ten you will find something that you need to clip, prune, or deadhead and you will have to go back inside to get your secateurs. Keep a spare pair on the kitchen windowsill and get into the habit of always taking them with you. Treat them like your best friend and, if you remember to clean them immediately after use, sharpen them regularly and oil them when required, they will never let you down.

Spider plants love the dry life

You will often hear 'non-gardeners' say how easy they find spider plants to look after and boast that they always forget to water them and still they grow. Well, they have a point! Keep spider plants as dry as possible and you can't go wrong. Brown tips to the leaves are the first signs of over watering. As tempted as you are to include them in your regular watering regime, don't!

Plants prefer a warm evening bath

Evening is by far the best time for watering plants. Some of them, however, are more sensitive to chills than others and watering with very cold water on a spring or autumn evening can cause growth-check problems. To avoid this, simply fill your watering cans in the morning and put them in the shed, greenhouse or garage. By evening the water will have warmed up and will be at a more acceptable temperature for your plants. If you were constantly given freezing cold baths you wouldn't be very happy would you?!

Cyclamen are fussy but fun

Cyclamen make beautiful houseplants and are particular favourites at Christmas when they will flower continuously through the winter. The cyclamen plant grows from a surface-planted corm, which particularly resents being watered from above and will soon rot if treated in this way. It also prefers tepid water and high humidity (fussy little devil isn't it?). Get into the habit of standing the plant pot in a saucer of wet clay granules to increase the humidity around the plants and, when it requires watering, stand in a dish of warm water for about 10 minutes. It is worth the hassle, honestly!

Quick-root cuttings

A jam jar of fresh water always kept on a sunny windowsill is the perfect place for rooting cuttings of many plants. Geraniums root easily in this way but so will many intended cuttings or even bit of broken plants that you find around the garden. Give it a try!

No more wobbly lines of carrots

A very easy way to make a perfectly straight seed drill in the vegetable patch is to use a 1" (2.5cm) diameter broom handle. First, prepare the soil to a level surface, firm with your feet and finish by lightly raking the top of the soil to loosen it. Then lay the broom handle onto the soil and press to the required depth. When removed, you have the perfect seed drill! Sowing the seeds over the whole diameter of the shallow drill left by the broom handle will create more space in which the plants can develop.

Give perennials the basket touch

A wire hanging basket placed upside down over emerging, tall-stemmed perennials makes a great support for the stems as they grow. No more unsightly canes to poke you in the eye! If you know that the perennials in question are a bit tender or you want to encourage some earlier growth then fill the upturned basket with autumn leaves in October or November. The basket will keep the leaves in place and you can simply remove them in spring when the danger of frost has passed.

Quick tip

LADDERED TIGHTS GIVE LOADS OF TIES!
Old laddered pairs of tights or stockings can be cut into thin strips to make ties for gentle climbers such as clematis as well as staked perennials. The stretching nature of the material allows for movement in the wind and unlike string and wire, it won't cut into delicate stems.

A rare spring bloom

Here's a fun tip to amaze your friends! In the autumn choose a nice, plump daffodil bulb. Next buy from the greengrocer a large, fresh beetroot. Cut the top off the beetroot, hollow it out and mash up the scooped out material with a little sunflower oil. Place the daffodil bulb inside the beetroot 'shell' and pack the mashed up beet around the bulb. Plant the whole thing in the garden, as you would a normal daffodil bulb. The result of your strange activity is pink daffodil flowers in spring as the plant takes up the beetroot dye into the petals. Try it but keep the admirers guessing as to how you did it.

Seed storage

Do you need to sow all the seeds in that packet or could you save some to sow next year? These days the viability of new seeds is much greater than it used to be so you probably don't have to sow all of them to obtain the number of plants you need. Unsown seeds can be saved by storing them, in a labelled paper envelope, in the fridge or freezer. Remember, though, that vegetable and herb seeds do have a 'sow by' date on the packet after which their viability will drop considerably. You will never, however, find a sow by date on a packet of flower seeds as they can potentially last forever if kept cool and dry. Proof of this was shown a few years ago when seeds of the Arctic lupin were found frozen in the ice at the edge of the Arctic Circle where they remained for over 10,000 years. When thawed and planted they germinated within a few days and grew into Arctic lupins identical to those that grow in that region today. If necessary Mother Nature will wait a while!

The longer I live
the greater is my
respect and affection
for manure in
all its forms.

Elizabeth von Arnim

Feeding & watering

chapter 2
Feeding & watering

Cowpat compost

Some gardening tips might seem a little odd and raise an
eyebrow of suspicion, but can really work well. This is one
such a beauty and the results are really are amazing ...

To keep the annual flowers in your hanging baskets and
containers looking wonderful, crumble up a dried cowpat
and mix into the compost before planting. Approximately half
a dinner plate sized pat is perfect for a 14" (35cm) basket or
tub. Wear gloves, of course, when applying the bovine bonanza
but you need not hold your breath as, amazingly, there is very
little smell.

Stinging nettles – saints or sinners?

Don't be too hasty in ridding your garden of every stinging
nettle you see. Many butterflies will only lay their eggs in
the protective stinging foliage of a nettle so leave a few around
to increase the numbers of these valuable pollinating insects.
Nettles are also packed full of nitrogen so any you do remove
will be prime fillet steak for the compost heap, helping to
activate the breakdown process and giving you much better
quality compost. In fact, actively look to scrounge nettles
from neighbours and friends for this purpose or grow your own.
People may think you are bonkers but you'll have the last laugh
with free, crumbly home-made compost.

"Gardening is a medicine that doesn't need a prescription ... and has no limit on dosage."

Anon

Steve's choice plants with scented leaves

When you are considering fragrance in the garden, don't just restrict yourself to scented flowers. There are countless plants whose leaves give off beautiful aromas when touched. Here are but a few …

- *Aloysia triphylla* (Lemon verbena)
- *Borago officinalis* (Borage)
- *Chamaemelum nobile* (Chamomile)
- *Choisya arizonica* 'Aztec Pearl' (Mexican orange blossom)
- *Foeniculum vulgare 'Purpureum'* (Bronze fennel)
- *Juniperus communis* (Juniper)
- *Laurus nobilis* (Bay tree)
- *Lavandula angustifolia* (Common lavender)
- *Melissa officinalis* (Lemon balm)
- *Mentha piperita* (Peppermint)
- *Mentha spicata* (Spearmint)
- *Nepeta faassenii* (Catmint)
- *Ocimum basilicum* (Basil)
- *Origanum vulgare* (Oregano)
- *Pelargonium crispum* (Lemon scented geranium)
- *Pelargonium tomentosum* (Peppermint geranium)
- *Salvia officinalis* (Sage)
- *Santolina chamaecyparissus* (Cotton lavender)
- *Teucrium chamaedrys* (Germander)
- *Thuja plicata* (Western red cedar)

Be a sucker for free tomato food

Tomato plants are hungry little devils and particularly fussy eaters. Apart from the normal plant foods they crave for trace elements and minerals such as iron, manganese, magnesium, calcium, copper, boron, and sulphur. These 'extras' give the plants and their fruit added health, quality, and taste as well as resistance to disease and nutrient deficiency symptoms. Trace element feeds are available from the garden centre but the best source for all of these requirements is hidden under your feet, and it's free – vacuum cleaner fluff!

When tested this weekly (or daily for the very house-proud) waste product contains all of these vital trace elements. "How come?" you might ask. Well think what might be in your vacuum cleaner back. Mainly it consists of bits of us – dead skin that we constantly shed – plus a mixture of dust, animal and human hair and millions of dead decaying dust mites. Yummy isn't it?! Well to a tomato plant it is a real energy boost. One handful per week gently mulched into the soil or compost at the base of the tomato plant gives amazing results – healthier plants as well as better tasting fruit with thinner skins and a resistance to splitting. This is one of those tips that really has got to be tried to be believed.

To prove to yourself that I really haven't lost the plot completely, next time you grow a crop of tomato plants feed them all as normal with your preferred tomato feed but around just one of them fork in a weekly mulch of the vacuum cleaner fluff. The results will be amazing!

Go bananas for roses

Roses are probably the hungriest plants in your garden and
when coming into flower they are looking for one particular
plant food – potassium. Proprietary rose feeds contain this,
as does the generic, straight feed, 'sulphate of potash'. But for
that added boost of potassium look no further than your fruit
bowl for the humble banana. The middle bit might be good
for us but the best bit for your roses is the skin – it is full of
potassium and more than any other fruit skin. Chop up the skins
into small pieces and fork them gently into the surface of the
soil at the base of the rose bush being careful not to disturb
the plant roots. As the banana skins quickly rot down they will
release their potassium into the soil in a form that the rose can
use immediately without waiting until it is mixed with other
chemicals in the soil. The result is better flowering with larger,
longer-lasting blooms, stronger scents, richer colours and
bigger, brighter hips. What more could you want?

Lime-hating plants pine for a mulch

The key to keeping lime-hating plants looking good is to acidify the soil. Special liquid feeds will do this but a good, natural way is to mulch around the plants with dead pine needles. Collect these on your weekend walks in the park, or from beneath friends' pine trees and put them to good use around your rhododendrons, azaleas etc ... No need to fork them in as eventually they will rot down.

Don't be sheepish – make your own liquid feed

One of the most rewarding gardening tasks is making your own plant food and saving yourself a fortune at the garden centre. Years ago my granddad used to stuff pigeon droppings collected from the floor of his pigeon loft into the foot ends of a pair of my grandmother's stockings. These 'smelly feet', as we called them, were then steeped in one special water butt for a couple of weeks to make a wonderful liquid plant feed for his whole garden. The prize-winning flowers and vegetables he grew were testament to the wonderful effect of his magic 'pigeon-poo' feed.

Today pigeons are not kept so much but a similar rich liquid feed can be achieved by using sheep droppings collected, perhaps, on a romantic Sunday stroll in the country. Simply repeat granddad's method for great results and the cost of just a pair of tights. Remember that these 'neat' animal manures are too strong to be used directly on the soil. Keep one water butt as your food factory and use every couple of weeks on your plants.

Now here's a wee tip!

If you want your compost heap to rot down really quickly and produce some tip-top compost, then male urine is what you want. Collect it in a bottle (ask first of course!), pour onto the heap immediately and mix into the top 6" (15cm) layer. It seems that there are chemicals, present only in male urine, that speed up the breakdown of plant material. Sorry ladies – can't use you here!

Climbing the food wall

A climbing plant planted at the base of a wall can often struggle to find the necessary food as it grows. A good tip is to actually pre-spray the wall with a liquid foliar feed before planting. As the plant grows it will obtain nourishment from the feed that has been absorbed in the wall's surface and put on much faster growth. Repeat the application every few weeks and the plant should never go hungry.

Simple slow-release feeding

An easy way to push those cone-shaped bundles of slow-release fertiliser pellets into hanging baskets and tubs is to first make a hole using an apple corer – it is just about the right size. You can then easily pop the plug of compost back in the hole after dropping in the slow-release pellets. This also stops you getting compost or soil deep under your nails.

Talking of dirty fingernails when gardening, try my tip on page 136 and you'll be laughing!

RECYCLING RABBITS

The straw from the weekly changes of the guinea pig or rabbit hutch can go straight into the bottom of the prepared trenches for peas and beans. A 2″ (5cm) layer of the straw, together with all the droppings, will give a much needed nitrogen-rich boost to the plants, as well as helping to conserve water in the soil.

Free iron-rich feed

Never throw away used tea bags. They can be used to make a great iron rich feed for your plants, particularly the acid loving ones such as rhododendrons, azaleas, pieris and skimmias. The extra iron will help to keep the leaves of these lime hating plants a beautiful dark green.

Keep a jug of water on the kitchen windowsill and drop the spent tea bags into it. At the end of the week you should have a jug full of dark brown liquid. Simply water this directly around your plants and then put the bags on the compost heap where they will rot down. The liquid feed also provides a much needed iron-rich top up for houseplants. If you don't fancy making the liquid feed then just break the tea bags open and mulch them into the soil at the base of your plants. The effect will be the same but not as instant.

A need for watering?

It is so easy to get the hose out and give everything in the garden a good drenching, but do all your plants really need it? A few minutes spent having a feel of the compost in tubs, or the soil under leaves of plants in the border might just reveal some that are actually OK for water. Apart from saving water this might also save harming those plants that actually prefer it a bit on the dry side.

A sooty watering

To intensify the colours of sweet pea flowers, water them around the roots with soot water when they are coming into bud. The results are amazing!

Get water to the root of the problem

If you grow plants, such as sunflowers, that require a good supply of water, then sink a 5" (12.5cm) plastic flowerpot alongside the plant at planting time. You can then water into the pot and be confidant that the majority of the water is going straight where it is needed – to the roots.

If, during a hot, dry spell of weather, you find that the water you give your plants doesn't seem to be getting to the roots then an old broom handle can come to your rescue. Carefully push the broom handle as deep as you can into dry soil around your plants. Then simply water into the holes made by the broom handle, confident the water will go straight to the roots of your plants.

Don't waste those excess drips!

Hanging baskets can dry out very quickly due to the effects of the sun and the wind. The rule of thumb is to water a hanging basket until excess water runs out of the bottom. Great advice but what happens to the excess water? It is wasted. A simple tip is to put an empty bucket under the basket before watering to collect the run off which can be used elsewhere.

Soaking solution for a dry basket

A quick and easy way to give a hanging basket a good soaking, after initial planting, is to hang it from a broom handle across the open top of a water butt or stand the basket on a large bucket. Only the bottom inch of the basket needs to be in the water for capillary action to water the whole basket. Usually about an hour is needed for the whole basket to become soaked. This is also a good tip to use should the basket get very dry at times during the summer, when normal watering from above just seems to run off the dry compost.

Stocking filter

Precious rainwater in a water butt can easily go sour if leaves are allowed to find their way into it via the inlet pipe and rot down. The simplest way to avoid this is to cover the end of the water down pipe that feeds into the water butt with the foot end part from a stocking or one leg of a pair of tights. This acts as a filter and collects the offending leaves. You must remember, though, to regularly clean out your homemade leaf filter.

Steve's choice plants for sunny, dry sites

Hot dry situations in the garden can prove difficult for any plant that is not adapted to cope. Plants, such as these below will thrive in these conditions having characteristics which are beautiful and practical ...

- *Anthemis tinctoria* (Yellow chamomile)
- *Cistus* 'Silver Pink' and 'Peggy Sammons'
- *Clianthus formosus* (Sturt's desert pea)
- *Cytisus multiflorus* (White Spanish broom)
- *Erysimum* 'Bowles Mauve' (Bowles' perennial wallflower)
- *Euryops pectinatus* (Bush daisy)
- *Festuca glauca* (Blue fescue)
- *Ficus carica* (Common fig)
- *Fritillaria imperialis* (Crown imperial)
- *Grevillea* 'Canberra Gem'
- *Lavandula dentata* (French lavender)
- *Papaver orientale* (Oriental poppy)
- *Phlomis fruticosa* (Jerusalem sage)
- *Phormium* 'Dazzler' (New Zealand flax)
- *Ruta graveolens* (Common rue)
- *Senecio cineraria* 'Silver Dust'
- *Sophora japonica* (Pagoda tree)
- *Verbena* 'Homestead Purple'
- *Verbena* 'Peaches and Cream'
- *Yucca filamentosa* (Adam's needle)

When weeding,
the best way to make
sure you are removing
weeds and not valuable
plants is to pull on it.
If it comes out of the
ground easily, it is
a valuable plant.

Anon

Weeds, pests & diseases

chapter 3
Weeds, pests & diseases

Roll on spot-weeder

The gardening industry loves you to spend money and tempts you with products that are frankly an unnecessary expense. Take the 'spot weeder' for the lawn. This is simply ordinary lawn weed killer in a fancy applicator. Don't buy one; make your own using an empty roll-on deodorant container. When the container is empty just prise off the ball, wash out well and fill, carefully whilst wearing gloves, with ordinary lawn weed killer diluted as per the manufacturer's instruction. Push the ball back on and, hey presto, you have your own roll-on weed killer for use on that odd lawn weed or when it is too windy to spray the lawn with weed killer. Oh, yes, do me a favour please and label it!

Quick tip

A PRETTY WHITEFLY DETERRENT

Get into the habit of always planting French marigolds alongside tomato plants – even in a hanging basket or window box. They will look very attractive but, more importantly, the smell given off by the marigolds is brilliant at deterring whitefly, a serious pest of tomatoes. The marigold variety 'Boy O Boy' seems to work best.

Keep cats at bay with tea bags & muscle spray

Cats! A word that can instil dread into many a gardener. Newly tilled soil is their perfect litter tray and the buried deposits are not a welcome find – especially if you don't wear gardening gloves! An easy way to keep cats away from any area of the garden is by drying out used tea bags and spraying them with a muscle rub spray, such as Ralgex or Deep Heat. Even a chemist's or supermarket's own brand spray will do the trick.

The tea bags can then be buried about ½" (12mm) deep over the soil area where the cats scratch, or left in those corners of the garden where the cats mark their territory. Three tea bags to every square yard should be enough. The cats hate the smell and will keep well away! Being oily, the muscle spray is not easily washed off by the rain and the deterrent will last for a good two weeks, by which time the cat has found another, more convenient, convenience.

Scary film for the birds

A single old, discarded videocassette can be easily recycled into hundreds of bird scarers to protect newly emerging seedlings all around the garden. Pull out 2' (60cm) lengths of the tape and tie to 3' (90cm) tall canes. The slightest breeze will blow the tape about to alarm the birds and the shiny side will reflect the light to further startle them.

Steve's top herbs for a summer hanging basket

Never think of a hanging basket as just a vehicle for displaying trailing plants and flowers. A herb basket can be a real winner just outside the back door.

- Basil – try lemon, lime and Thai varieties (not hardy)
- Chervil
- Chives
- Coriander (not hardy)
- Dill – fern-leaf variety
- Garlic chives
- Lemon Balm
- Mint – try apple, pineapple or ginger varieties
- Nasturtiums (not strictly a herb but edible leaves & flowers!)
- Oregano
- Parsley – flat leaved varieties have more flavour
- Rosemary (in centre – move when too large)
- Sage – variegated
- Tarragon
- Thyme – try common and lemon varieties

The basket will need at least 4 hours of sun each day – more if possible. Try to shelter the basket from the wind. Use good, free-draining compost and if you are using herbs like mint or basil, you'll want a pretty fertile mixture so mix in some slow release fertilizer. The Mediterranean herbs such as rosemary, thyme or sage need a little sand or grit added for extra drainage in the bottom of their planting holes.

" The philosopher who said that "work well done never needs doing again" obviously never weeded a garden. "

Anon

Brush up your pond

Blanket weed in a pond can be a nightmare to remove and you can spend hours trying to scoop it out. The quick and easy solution is to buy a cheap, round hairbrush and tie this firmly to a long pole or bamboo cane. Push the hairbrush into the weed and twist round and round. The weed neatly wraps itself around the brush allowing you to remove it completely. Even if there isn't any weed visible on the surface, a weekly rolling of the brush just below the pond surface can remove the start of any blanket weed problems. Always be careful, of course, not to harm any fish or established pond plants.

Rose, mint and garlic harmony!

Planting a combination of mint and wild garlic between roses has a double benefit. The invasive mint smothers any weeds but won't compete adversely with the strong growing and hungry roses and the garlic emits a smell that deters greenfly. Incredibly the three types of plants seem to grow quite happily together.

The pleasures of weeding

Weeding is one of the most rewarding and enjoyable of gardening practices. It often gets you on your hands & knees and close to the soil where you will see all manner of amazing things that might otherwise have gone unnoticed. Newly emerging seedlings of self-set perennial and annual seeds can often reveal themselves along with a myriad of soil creatures – some good, some bad.

Couch grass cleared by territorial tomatoes!

This is another one of those tips that works but no one really knows why. If your garden has a patch of couch grass that is proving difficult to get rid of, then simply sow some cheap tomato seeds in the middle of it in early spring. The tomato seedlings will grow and the couch grass will have disappeared. It seems the two can't compete and the tomato plants win – every time. Some scientists think that a chemical produced by the tomato plant roots kills the couch grass. Who cares – as long as it works?!

Quick tip

WEEDING TWEEZERS
Weeding in between delicate seedlings and around the base of fragile potted plants can be a tricky job. Using a pair of eyebrow tweezers makes the job a whole lot easier.

Ponds get the short straw

Green algae infested water in your pond is not an attractive sight. There is no need to try an array of chemicals to solve the problem; all you need is some barley straw. Small, handy-size bales are available from many garden centres or you can make your own with some barley straw and some plastic garden netting. Just toss the bale into the pond and let nature do the work. A chemical given off by the barley straw in the water will kill off the algae whilst causing no harm to the pond's wildlife.

Steve's top slug and snail proof perennials

Are you constantly losing the battle against slugs and snails? If so, give yourself a break and grow something they won't touch ...

- *Aconitum carmichaelii* 'Arendsii'
- *Allium* 'Globemaster' (Ornamental onion)
- *Artemesia ludoviciana* (Western mugwort)
- *Arum italicum* 'Marmoratum' (Lords and ladies)
- *Aster ericoides* 'Esther'
- *Bergenia species* (Elephant's ears)
- *Campanula percicifolia* (Peach-leaved bellflower)
- *Colchium* 'Waterlily' (Autumn crocus)
- *Corydalis lutea*
- *Epimedium pinnatum* (Barrenwort)
- *Galanthus species* (Snowdrop)
- *Geranium macrorrhizum* (Cranesbill)
- *Helleborus foetidus* (Bear's foot)
- *Helleborus x nigercors*
- *Hosta* 'Halcyon' (Plantation lily)
- *Iris chrysographes*
- *Lobelia siphilitica* (Blue cardinal flower)
- *Pulmonaria angustifolia* (Blue cowslip)
- *Rudbeckia hirta* (Black-eyed Susan)
- *Sedum telephium* 'Matrona' (Ice plant)

Say goodbye to holey hostas

It probably seems that whatever slug and snail protection you put around the hostas growing in your flower border, they still get decimated. Well firstly, the slug and snail barrier that you are using, be it broken egg shells, grit, soot etc.., is working just fine. The problem will have started in the previous autumn. When your old hosta leaves were dying off, being a good gardener, you left the leaves to go completely brown so that all the goodness could return to the root stock of the plant. Then you removed the dead leaves and your hostas went to ground for their winter rest. What you had probably not realised was that under those dying leaves, before you removed them, slugs and snails had found the ideal protective humid nesting ground, and had been happily reproducing and burying their eggs in the soil at the base of your hostas.

When spring arrives you diligently and speedily put your barriers around the newly emerging hosta shoots. Then all the buried eggs begin to hatch and the newly-emerged slugs and snails can't escape because you have succeeded in trapping them in with your protective measures. Why should they care? They have been born in McDonalds! As soon as you see signs of the spring shoots appearing, you should remove and dispose of a ring of egg-laden soil, 2" (5cm) deep by 12" (30cm) diameter from around the plants. Replace this immediately with fresh compost and your chosen slug and snail prevention. Job done!

A two-pronged attack for an ant free existence

Ants are perhaps the most disliked of any garden pest because they have the audacity to come into your house as well! Try as you may with regular ant powders, they never seem to do the whole job. That's because they kill by contact and although the ants on the surface succumb, the real culprit is sitting pretty in her protective subterranean domain – the queen. She is happily churning out new ants to replace those you kill above ground at a rate of thousands a day. Killing her is the secret to a respite from annoying ants because if she dies the colony cannot survive. Killing the queen, though, isn't easy. Firstly she is fed by the worker ants who will not feed her anything they realise would be dangerous to her.

The trick is to dupe the ants into feeding the queen poison by lacing it with the one thing that disrupts their senses and sends them into ant heaven – sugar. The poison to use is the one thing that is certain death to an ant – naturally occurring borax, available in crystal form as a laundry cleaning aid. Mix one part sugar with one part borax crystals and sprinkle where you can see the ants appearing. The borax sticks to the sugar and the ants are oblivious to its presence. Ants are not allowed to eat until they have fed the queen so they happily stuff her full of the mixture and she quickly expires. Now the colony is in complete disarray without a queen. The ants soon coming running out of the nest, which is when you knock them off with ant powder, or an anteater if you want to be really environmentally friendly!

Egg-actly the right home for ladybirds

Ladybirds are one of the garden's most useful predatory insects and will happily feed for hours on troublesome greenfly. To ensure that ladybirds are resident in your garden from early spring, you need to provide them with a safe haven in which to over-winter. The best thing is an old egg box, opened out and pushed, upside down, into a hedge, under a shed or somewhere else where it will be relatively dry and undisturbed through the winter months. The ladybirds will find the egg compartments both warm, dry, and a safe refuge from predators.

Garlic is a real turn off for broad bean blackfly

Garlic has some wonderful culinary and medicinal uses for us and your garden can benefit as well. A few cloves planted in between rows of broad beans will deter blackfly – the vampire pests of broad bean plants, sucking the sap out of the succulent new shoots. You won't smell the garlic unless the leaves are crushed but the nasally-superior blackfly will get an immediate whiff and will soon depart.

Assault those despicable dandelions

If you want to get rid of those odd, annoying dandelions in your lawn but don't want to spray with weed killer or risk breaking them off underground by trying to pull them out, then a little table salt poured into the centre of the plant will do the trick. This will slowly burn out the heart of the weed within a day or so.

The gloves are on for troublesome weeds

Some weeds are just impossible to get rid of without a bit of chemical help, unless you are able to take away areas of soil so the whole root system can be removed. Bindweed, mare's-tail and ground elder fall into this category. Breaking them off at the soil surface exacerbates the problem as the roots just produce many more plants from the broken stem. Control requires the use of a glyphosate-based herbicide. Glyphosate works systemically by travelling through the plant to kill the root. When in contact with the soil it is rendered harmless. These attributes make glyphosate the most environmentally friendly of the weed killers available. The trouble is that it will kill any green plant that it comes in contact with which makes using it in between other plants a challenge.

The answer is quite simple. First make up a solution of glyphosate-based weed killer in a bucket. Then put on a new rubber glove followed by an old woollen glove or sock over the top. Dip this hand into the solution and squeeze out any excess liquid. Now carefully reach through your plants, take hold of the offending weed, and let it run through your gloved hand. Enough weed killer solution will be on the weed for the glyphosate to take effect without harming your other plants. To deal really effectively with bindweed, as soon as you notice it place a short bamboo cane in the soil next to the plant and train it up the cane over the following weeks. Then your gloved weed-killing job is made much easier. Be sure to discard the used woolly glove safely and carefully or wash it extremely well in warm soapy water before using again.

Vine weevil temptation

Without doubt the best way to cure a vine weevil problem is to employ a biological control such as Nemasys. This consists of using parasitic nematodes to kill the vine weevil larvae in the soil. Unfortunately this control has no effect on the vine weevil adults, which can still lay more eggs.

There is, however, a neat way of clearing the adults out of the soil before using a biological control. All you need is a 3" (7.5cm) diameter plastic pot, a handful of damp barley straw and an old carrier bag. In the evening fill the pot with the damp straw and place it, on its side, on top of the pot or container from which you want to remove the vine weevil adults. Leave it in place until the following morning when you need to tip the contents of the pot into the carrier bag. In the damp straw you should find a number of soil pests including woodlice, earwigs and, of course, the vine weevils. How does it work? Well, damp barley straw gives of a gas that attracts these creatures out of the soil. You might have to do this over a few nights to be sure of getting rid of all the vine weevil adults. Then you can use your biological control on the larvae.

Puss off!

Cats love to roll around on newly planted seed beds. Stop them by sticking some prickly twigs such as holly or berberis in the soil over the area you want to protect.

"Make no mistake,
the weeds will win –
nature bats last.

Anon

Steve's top rabbit-proof shrubs

Even shrubs are not always safe from a hungry bunny.
The following shrubs, however, are not palatable to rabbits
so use these as perimeter plants along with the herbaceous
perennials on page 85 ...

- *Arundinaria species* (Bamboo)
- *Buxus sempervirens* (Box)
- *Ceanothus thyrisiflorus var. repens*
- *Cornus sanguinea* 'Winter Beauty' (Common dogwood)
- *Cotoneaster horizontalis*
- *Fuchsia* species
- *Gaultheria mucronata* 'Mulberry Wine' (Prickly heath)
- *Hypericum calycinum* (Rose of Sharon)
- *Kalmia latifolia* (Calico bush)
- *Laurus nobilis* (Bay)
- *Lonicera species* (Honeysuckle)
- *Prunus laurocerasus* (Cherry laurel)
- *Rhododendron* species
- *Rosa* 'Rosy Cushion' (Shrub rose)
- *Rosmarinus officinalis* (Rosemary)
- *Ruscus aculeatus* (Butcher's broom)
- *Sambucus nigra* (Golden elder)
- *Skimmia japonica*
- *Spirea japonica* 'Anthony Waterer'
- *Vinca species* (Periwinkle)

Felt collars stop slugs and snails

Slugs and snails feature a lot in this book! Squares of green mineral roofing felt – the type on your garden shed roof – is a great way of ensuring that the slimy pests can't reach your plants. Cut a hole in the middle of a 6" (15cm) square of the felt, wide enough to fit around the plant stem. Now cut a slit halfway across to enable you to slip the square, like a collar, around the plant. There are two reasons why slugs and snails are loath to traverse the felt. Firstly the surface is very rough which hurts their underbellies, and secondly, they appear to hate the smell of the bitumen glue in the felt, especially on a warm summer's evening.

As with many attempts at beating the slugs and snails you must adopt a 'belt and braces' approach and the same applies here. As well as making a collar of the mineral felt you could leave a larger hole for fitting around the plant and then fill this gap with sharp grit or gravel or crushed eggshells. If any of the enemy do make it across the rough felt then your second line of defence might save the day!

Quick tip

TELLTALE ONION TIPS
Prevent birds from pulling your onion sets out of the ground by simply cutting off the dead tips of the sets before planting. It is these tips that the birds have developed a mischievous eye for so without them visible, the birds should leave your onion sets alone.

An organic solution to rose mildew

Mildew on roses is often a difficult disease to control unless you want to resort to frequent chemical sprayings. Try this old tip – it's worked on many occasions and is totally organic …

Mix 1 tablespoon of baking powder with ¼ pint of milk and add a teaspoon of sunflower oil. Stir thoroughly and pour into a hand sprayer. Liberally coat both sides of the leaves of the affected rose. The baking powder and the milk are the effective ingredients and the oil just helps the mixture stick to the leaves.

Rose mildew spores prefer the slightly acid surface of rose leaves. This milk and baking powder mixture will be absorbed onto the surfaces of the leaves and will make them alkaline – a condition that the mildew spores detest. When the mixture has dried completely the unsightly white staining can be easily washed off with water. Enough of the mix will have entered the leaves to be effective.

Ready-salted cabbages?

Avoid the devastating effect of caterpillars munching through the leaves of your brassicas by watering the young plants with a dilute table salt solution. One tablespoon to two gallons (9 litres) of water will be sufficient. The salt is taken into the plant leaves making them unpalatable for caterpillars. As the plants mature, the salt will be lost from the leaves so the edible brassicas won't be tainted.

Pot protection

Even plants in containers are not safe from the nocturnal nibbling of hungry slugs and snails. Preventing them from actually reaching the object of their desire – your prize plants – is easier than you think. A 2″ (5cm) wide barrier around the pot is usually enough. To make this barrier use either Vaseline (petroleum jelly), WD-40 (the water repellent spray), or double sided sticky tape. If using the spray ensure that you protect the plants with newspaper before applying. The slugs and snails don't like the stickiness of the Vaseline or tape and they seem to hate the WD-40.

Now here's a bit of useless but interesting information. Have you ever wondered how WD-40 got its name? Well, the spray was originally developed in 1953 as a corrosion protection for space rockets. The manufacturers were apparently struggling to find a suitable name so they decided on WD-40. WD stands for 'water displacement' and 40 for the forty attempts it took to get it right. Talk about persistence!

Quick tip

IMMEDIATE ACTION
Question: When should you pull out a weed?
Answer: As soon as you see it – most people don't!

Some weeds have such short life-cycles that even leaving it a day could mean the production of more weed seeds.

Lacewing and ladybird log cabin

For a natural balance in your garden you need to attract beneficial insects to help keep the pests under control. A bundle of 6" (15cm) lengths of hollowed out bamboo canes and put in any sheltered place – under a shed or in a hedge – provides a brilliant home for over wintering lacewings and ladybirds, two of the most useful predators of aphids.

Wash day blues for slugs and snails

A short-lived but very effective deterrent for slugs and snails is washing powder. Keep a box of the cheap, supermarket own brand sort for those emergencies when you have none of the other more permanent items from other tips in this book. A handful of washing powder around a susceptible plant will stop the little devils by clogging up their slime glands. They are literally stopped in their tracks. Amusingly, if you venture outside with a torch after dark, you will be able to find the stranded slugs and snails quite easily as in their efforts to escape the excess slime they produce will often make tell-tale bubbles of soap! Unfortunately, after the first shower of rain the powder is lost, so treat it as a temporary and entertaining measure.

Mulch ado

Mulching around your roses with well-rotted lawn clippings in early spring, just before leaf break, will help prevent black spot. It has been shown that chemicals produced by the rotted grass can kill the black spot spores.

Steve's top rabbit-proof perennials

Most of your herbaceous perennials can be breakfast, lunch, dinner and supper to a rabbit. Fox them by growing some of the following around the perimeter of your garden together with the shrubs mentioned on page 76 – they won't touch them and might just hop off elsewhere ...

- *Agapanthus* 'Blue Giant' (African lily)
- *Aconitum* 'Blue Sceptre' (Monskshood)
- *Alchemilla Mollis* (Lady's Mantle)
- *Anemone x hybrida* (Windflower)
- *Aquilegia vulgaris* (Columbine)
- *Aster novi-belgi* (Michaelmas daisy)
- *Bergenia species* (Elephant's ears)
- *Convallaria majalis* (Lily of the valley)
- *Crocosmia* 'Lucifer' (Montbretia)
- *Digitalis pupurea* (Foxglove)
- *Euphorbia griffithii* 'Fireglow' (Spurge)
- *Helleborus hybridus* (Lenten rose)
- *Kniphofia triangularis* (Red hot poker)
- *Lamium maculatum* 'Beacon Silver' (Dead nettle)
- *Narcissus species* (Daffodil)
- *Nepeta faassenii* (Catmint)
- *Paeonia officianalis* (Peony)
- *Pulmonaria saccharata* (Jerusalem sage)
- *Sedum telephium* 'Matrona' (Ice plant)
- *Trollius x cultorum* (Globeflower)

"I appreciate the misunderstanding I have had with Mother Nature over my perennial border. I think it is a flower garden; she thinks it is a meadow lacking grass, and tries to correct the error.

Sara Stein

Clean off those pests

A multi-purpose, environmentally friendly plant spray against a range of pests can be made by saving up all those scraps of soap you have left in the bathroom or kitchen. When you have enough, boil up 2 tablespoons of the soap bits with ½ gallon (2.25 litres) of water. When all of the soap has dissolved, allow the solution to cool and then give any pest-affected plants a good spray. This should kill enough of the pests to give the plants a fighting chance for a full recovery.

Deflate cats with a bit of inflation!

Sometimes with cats you have to take quite extreme measures to keep them from depositing in your freshly dug soil. You might have an area that you have prepared for planting a few days later. Left undefended next door's tom is likely to leave you a soft, smelly offering before the day's out. Here's a neat trick to try that will ensure he will never foul your flowerbeds again.

When you have finished preparing the soil dig a hole about 8" (20cm) deep and across. Now blow up a balloon so that it will just fit into the hole and sit below the soil surface (you are probably way ahead of me by now!). Now carefully fill in the hole around and over the balloon, sit back and enjoy the show!

I must add at this point that I am a cat lover. In fact, at the time of writing our lovely ginger cat, Fizz, has just had a litter of kittens. So I must explain that the above tip was actually given to me by a sweet Women's Institute lady when I was giving a talk to a WI Federation meeting. Obviously her view of cats is not as loving as mine!

Warty good idea!

Slugs and snails can decimate a strawberry patch of fruit overnight. A good, natural solution is to use one of nature's most voracious nocturnal hunters – the toad! Securely net off your strawberry bed and introduce a toad into the netted area. By ensuring that he cannot escape and that there is always a bowl of fresh water available, your warty friend will happily remain there all summer, making short work of the slugs and snails. Thankfully, toads are carnivores so he will leave the juicy strawberries alone.

If you don't have a pond and therefore find it difficult to locate your toad then either find someone who has a well-established pond or advertise in the local press and hire one for the season – in return for a bowl of strawberries perhaps!

Scary CDs

Have you had a good look at your junk mail recently? You will probably find that you are throwing out countless promotional CDs, which make excellent bird scarers! When hung by fine fishing line or twine over seed beds, fruit bushes and in fruit trees the birds are deterred when the reflective surfaces of the CDs give sudden flashes of light as they spin in the breeze. The birds won't disappear from your garden completely – just from the areas that you choose.

If you are having trouble finding any CDs to use then a visit to the shops might help. Many of the large retailers have their own brand of internet connection software available free on CDs at the checkouts. Need I say more?

Mirrors give carrot root fly a real headache!

This is one of those 'unbelievable-but-true' tips! Carrot root fly can devastate a crop and you can be oblivious to it until you start to pull the roots and see the damage that the larvae have done. This tip was given to me some years back by an old and, it seems, a very wise gardener.

There is hope in combating carrot root fly and it's all to do with finding out about the enemy. The female carrot root fly is the problem. She flies along the row of carrots at a height of about 1½ " (4cm) above the soil with a territory length of just over a yard (90cm). Before she lays her eggs, she will ensure that other carrot root flies do not infiltrate her patch by flying up and down her patch viciously attacking any that she sees. That is her Achilles heel! By standing old handbag mirrors back to back at just under one-yard (90cm) intervals along the row of carrots, the female carrot root fly will, amazingly, attack her reflection and keep up the attack until she drops dead at the base of the mirror. Neat trick eh?!

Defensive rings

Cut into 3" (7.5cm) wide rings, empty plastic pop bottles make great slug and snail guards for small susceptible plants. Carefully push the rings over the plants and about an inch into the soil. The sharp plastic edge is usually enough to stop the slugs and snails from breaching this cheap but effective defence. Filling in around the plant stem with an extra deterrent, such as sharp grit or broken eggshells, will double the protection.

SOOT CAN SWEEP AWAY SOIL PESTS!

Many soil pests on the vegetable plot can be deterred by raking soot into the soil surface at sowing time. This works particularly well for carrot root fly. If you don't have an open fire yourself, then scrounge some from a friend or neighbour. It'll be worth the effort.

Stomach ache for slugs and snails

Natural looking slug and snail deterrents are the best, and horsehair looks the part and works a treat. Stables get rid of huge quantities every week so you can easily scrounge some. Place it in a 4" (10cm) diameter ring around susceptible plants and weight down with one or two stones. Make sure, though, that the stones don't form a bridge to the plant. Slugs and snails cannot crawl over the hair for two reasons – the hair is an irritant, which they detest, but more importantly the horse grease on the hair reacts with their slime to form an acid that burns their underbellies. Have you ever seen a horse covered in snails? Well there you are then.

Steve's favourite trees for the smaller garden

If you love trees but have a small garden don't despair.
I promise that there is a suitable tree for you! Have a look
at these and be spoiled for choice …

- *Acer griseum* (Paper bark maple)
- *Acer pensylvanicum* (Snakeskin bark maple)
- *Aesculus pavia 'Atrosanguinea'* (Dark red buckeye)
- *Amelanchier lamarkii or Amelanchier laevis* (Snowy mespilus)
- *Aralia elata* (Japanese angelica tree)
- *Arbutus unedo* (Strawberry tree)
- *Betula pendula* 'Fastigiata' (Silver birch)
- *Cornus florida* 'Spring Song' (Flowering dogwood)
- *Corylus avellana* 'Contorta' (Corkscrew hazel)
- *Crataegus persimilis* 'Prunifolia' (Hawthorn)
- *Laburnum alpinum* (Scots laburnum)
- *Malus* 'Red Jade' or *Malus* 'John Downie' (Crab apple)
- *Malus domestica* 'Katja' (Desert apple)
- *Prunus* 'Kursar' (Ornamental cherry)
- *Prunus x subhirtella* 'Autumnalis' (Winter cherry)
- *Prunus subhirtella* 'Pendula Rubra' (Weeping spring cherry)
- *Pyrus salicifolia* 'Pendula' (Weeping pear)
- *Rhus trichocarpa* (Sumach)
- *Salix matsudana* 'Tortuosa' (Corkscrew willow)
- *Sorbus hostii* (Mountain ash)

Sunny hoverfly heaven

The hoverfly is one of the most useful insects in your garden because both the adults and the larvae are voracious eaters of greenfly. In fact the hoverfly will actively look for colonies of greenfly in which to lay its eggs. Yellow flowers are a great attraction for this friendly predator, which likes to hover at different levels in the garden looking for nectar on which to feed. Don't confuse the hoverfly with a wasp. You will instantly recognise their unique 'hovering' technique as they move up and down to different levels – just like an elevator – stopping for a while to see what's on offer.

The best way to keep hoverflies in your garden is to plant different heights of sunflowers from 'Dwarf Yellow Spray' at 18" (46cm) right up to the massive 'Russian Giant' at more than 10' (3m). You will benefit from the fabulous flowers; the antics of the birds and squirrels trying to get the seeds in the autumn; but best of all – you will have your very own built in greenfly control!

"Gardening seems to consist of greed and indigestion. Greed because you can't resist buying a plant and indigestion because there is no more room for it.

Christopher Wells

Soap will clean up a squirrel situation

A gardener's life can easily turn into a running battle with the squirrel. Cute when they are performing their acrobatics atop your fence or in a tree but not so cute when they are doing so with one of your fat, juicy crocus bulbs in their mouth! Accept the fact that you will have to live with nature's prettiest rodent and try appeasing its appetite by leave some over ripe apples as a sign of your offer of truce. Then protect all your planted bulbs with the best squirrel deterrent there is – grated soap – the cheaper and more smelly the better. Squirrels hate the smell of it and will avoid it like the plague. Simply grate up the soap and sprinkle over the surface of the soil where you have planted any bulbs. You might have to re-apply after rain but soap is cheap enough and should last you all season.

So why should this work? Have squirrels an aversion for personal hygiene? No, not as far as I know, but a main constituent of soap – stearic acid – does produce an allergic reaction in our furry friend that is similar to hay fever. It doesn't hurt the squirrel but it does ensure that it keeps away from any area where you apply the grated soap. Grating simply increases the surface area of the soap so you get a better effect. Perhaps I should also say that it is better to not use the normal cheese grater from the kitchen! Far better to buy a cheap one from a market or discount store to use just for this tip.

This tip will also work to keep squirrels off the bird table. Simply cut soap into cubes, make a hole through the middle of each cube and string them together. Hang the 'soap-on-a-rope' squirrel deterrent on the bird table and the birds should be able to luncheon in peace!

Shocked into submission

Snails are the mountaineers of the garden and boy can they climb! If 30ft up a laburnum tree is no big deal for them then a couple of feet up the side of your hosta pot is an evening stroll to a walk-through McDonalds! Elsewhere in this tome of terrific tips are other ideas to keep slugs and snails away from your plants but this tip is shocking – literally! Read on ...

Take two thin strands of copper wire. Florist shops have the perfect thing or cheap, electrical doorbell cable with the plastic coating stripped off will work just fine. Tightly tie the wires around the pot, approximately ½" (13mm) apart. There must be no gaps for the little devils to squeeze under! Then, in the evening, go and find yourself a snail. Place the snail on the pot and watch it climb. This may take some time but it is well worth waiting for. When the unsuspecting snail crawls over the first copper wire – no problem. Then, with its bum on the first wire its front end will touch the second wire. Immediately a small electric current is set up by the reaction between the snail slime and the copper and the snail gets a shock and falls off the pot. Hilarious fun for all the family!

Quick tip

PINK PROTECTION
Epsom salts sprinkled around dianthus plants ('pinks') will keep the rabbits away.

Stop moles from ferreting around

There are few garden pests that cause more devastation to a well-kept lawn or border than the unassuming mole. I say unassuming because the little fellow is only a few inches in length and really doesn't mean to cause you such stress. He is just going about his normal daily business, which includes digging up your lawn, and leaving hills of freshly moved soil! Don't even consider killing him. That is barbaric. Instead use a natural approach.

The smell of the dung of a predator is usually more than enough to scare off most animals. The natural predator of the mole is the badger but it is notoriously difficult to get badger pooh! Luckily a close relative of the badger is the ferret and poor old Mr Mole, despite his acute sense of smell, can't seem to tell the difference. It is somewhat easier to obtain ferret droppings, as members of local ferret associations are only too happy to part with the stuff! Once obtained mix with a little water to make a paste, dig out the mole hill until you find the run and paint the ferret-pooh paste around the rim of the entrance, or put a small mound just inside. The wind will take the smell of the ferret down the hole, the mole will get a whiff, think "badger!" and scarper as quick as his paddle-feet will take him – never to darken your garden gate again.

Pass on this tip to the green-keeper at your local golf club and you will have a friend for life. There are at least three golf clubs that I know of that use this mole remedy and have regular deliveries of ferret dung. I'm glad I'm not their postman.

Oh dear! Another smelly tip!

Deer are best enjoyed at a distance; certainly not up close whilst they rip your prize plants to bits. Keeping deer, foxes and badgers out of your garden can be done but it does mean resorting to something smelly. Strips of material, or old rags soaked in household ammonia and hung in a net at the boundary point where you know these animals enter your garden will certainly do the trick. After a few weeks they will associate the area with the nasty smell and will avoid it.

An alternative to using ammonia solution, is to use strong male urine (sorry girls – yours just won't do!). It is not quite as pungent as the ammonia but deer are put off by the presence of what they think is a dominant male. So, if you consider yourself a real stag, guys – get weeing!

Kitty won't be sitting pretty

Cats can be easily persuaded to avoid using your newly planted seed trays, patio pots and window boxes as convenient loo stops. Simply pepper the surface of the compost with cocktail sticks, leaving about 3/4" (2cm) protruding. Listen out – the cat will only try it once – and when it comes down off the shed roof it will find somewhere else to take a loo break. Take care, of course, if you have small children around as the cocktail sticks can be quite sharp (if in doubt – ask the cat!). After a couple of weeks the cat will always associate the particular tub or container with, well, you can imagine, and will always avoid it. You don't, therefore, have to keep the cocktail sticks in place permanently.

Blackspot blues

Roses are lovely flowers but the plants are often susceptible to blackspot. Obviously you want to avoid excessive spraying all through the season so you diligently follow the spray manufacturer's instructions and spray as soon as the leaf buds break. Let me tell you a secret – you are about a week too late! You can reduce the amount of times that you need to spray roses against blackspot by spraying the plant when the buds swell but before they break, ensuring that the spray gets into the stem joints, to kill any over-wintering disease spores. Also spray the soil around the rose bush to a diameter of about 12" (25cm), again to kill any spores. If you fail to spray the soil, any blackspot spores will be bounced up onto the plant during the first heavy spring show of rain.

If you have a rose bush that you know always get badly infected with blackspot then carefully remove and dispose of a circle of the soil, 2" (5cm) deep, from around the rose bush to a diameter just beyond the spread of the plant. This is best done before pruning. This removed soil will contain millions of blackspot spores. Replace it with fresh compost and a mulch of bark chippings.

Another good way of keeping the spread of blackspot down is to instigate an almost obsessive hygiene regime when dealing with infected plants. Invest in a box of cheap, latex gloves similar to those worn by surgeons. When removing blackspot infected leaves from around your roses always wear a pair of these gloves and be really careful not to touch any other, healthy rose. Dispose of the gloves, with the infected leaves, in a rubbish sack after use.

Beer beats bacteria

Houseplants can often become the most neglected plants, especially when the seasonal emphasis is on the garden outside. Foliage houseplants in particular suffer because the pores of their leaves get blocked – not just with dust but also with bacteria. In order to grow healthily, a plant's leaves must breathe through their pores and exchange gases. Blocked pores means the plant could slowly choke to death. Cleaning the leaves with leaf wipes may make them shine but it does nothing to kill this bacteria. Help is at hand, however, with the best anti-bacterial cleaner for plant leaves – beer. The weak acid in beer will successfully kill the harmful bacteria clogging up the leaf the pores. A weekly clean of both sides of the leaves with cotton wool soaked in beer will do the trick and get your plants breathing more easily.

Citrus appeal

Slug pellets are fast becoming a real no-no for the environmentally concerned gardener. If you can, catch slugs and snails and remove them from your garden to somewhere where they can munch away without causing you stress. A good way to catch them is to place hollowed out half shells of large oranges and grapefruits around your garden borders in the evening. During the night the smell of the fruit will lure the slugs and snails inside where they will remain waiting for you to collect them in the morning. You will need to cut either a small doorway into the fruit shell or stand then on a couple of stones so they can gain easy access to their midnight citrus feast. This tip also encourages you to eat more fruit, which isn't a bad thing!

"In gardens, beauty is a by-product. The main business is sex and death.

Sam Llewelyn

A juicy solution to dog dead grass!

Nothing will kill grass faster than dog urine, especially that of the bitch dog. No matter how fast you are with a bucket of water to dilute the offending dog wee (or throw over the offending dog) it still seems to be strong enough to produce those telltale dead patches. Extra feeding of the grass also has little effect.

Well, forget the lawn itself, because the answer lies with the dog and its relationship with a bottle of tomato juice. Twice a day mix 1½ tablespoons of tomato juice with the dog's food – once in the morning, once in the evening. The reason for the timing is all to do with the working of the dog's bladder. Amazingly the tomato juice neutralises the chemical in the dog's urine that kills the grass. The dog can then wee all over the lawn as much as it wants with no ill effects to the grass. Unfortunately you have to keep up the dosage of juice every single day to maintain the effect. And it will only work, of course, with your dog. Convincing a neighbouring dog owner to do the same might just be asking too much. Umm ... Maybe slab the garden instead ...

Crowded house

For a gardener with little time on their hands the best way to keep the weeds down is to keep planting. The more you plant the more difficult it is for the weeds to get a foothold. Try to plant for a succession of interest with plants that come into their best (and hence take energy from the soil) at different times of the year. This enables you to plant closer to crow out the weeds and get maximum satisfaction from the results.

Steve's choice plants for dry, shady sites

The combination of shade and drought presents a challenge but the following plants will be able to tolerate this situation of lack of light and moisture …

- *Bergenia Sunningdale* (Elephant's ears)
- *Brunnera macrophylla* (Perennial forget-me-not)
- *Buxus sempervirens* (Common box)
- *Convallaria majalis* 'Rosea' (Lily of the valley)
- *Cotoneaster cornubia*
- *Digitalis* (Foxglove)
- *Euonymus fortunei* 'Silver Queen'
- *Euphorbia amygdaloides* (Spurge)
- *Garrya elliptica* (Silk tassel bush)
- *Hedera canariensis* (Canary Island ivy)
- *Hedera helix* 'Erecta' (English ivy)
- *Helleborus foetidus* (Stinking hellebore)
- *Hypericum calycinum* (Rose of Sharon)
- *Iris foetidissima*
- *Liriope muscari* 'Monroe White'
- *Lonicera pileata* (Privet honeysuckle)
- *Mahonia aquifolium* (Oregon grape)
- *Osmanthus delavayi* (Delavay tea olive)
- *Ribes alpinum* (Alpine currant)
- *Ruscus aculeatus* (Butcher's broom)

- *Sarcococca confusa* (Sweet box)
- *Symphoricarpos species* (Snowberry)
- *Taxus baccata* (English yew)
- *Vinca species* (Periwinkle)
- *Waldsteinia ternata*

There is no spot
of ground, however
arid, bare or ugly,
that cannot be tamed
into such a state as
may give an impression
of beauty and delight.

Gertrude Jekyll

Soils & situations

chapter 4
Soils & situations

Take a look at the origins of your species

You don't need a degree in botany to be able to grow a range of plants from around the world – just a good atlas. With detailed knowledge of the countries from which the plants originate you can mimic their natural growing conditions and achieve greater success. Lavender and many other herbs, for instance, come from a Mediterranean climate, so full sun and sandy, free draining soil is the order of the day.

Stop acting on impulse

We have all done it – me included. An innocent visit to the garden centre or nursery to buy a bag of compost results in the unwitting acquisition of a boot full of new plants that you just couldn't resist. So do you know where you are going to plant them? Do you heck as like! You will end up trying to squeeze them into places in the garden where they might struggle to survive and look good for a year but then things get too crowded, or the position just isn't quite right, and they die. Try at all costs to resist this temptation. Instead look around your garden and identify spaces that really do need to be planted. Make notes of the soil pH, drainage, aspect, space for future growth etc. that each plant needs to satisfy, and then make a definite visit to the garden centre to buy plants that you actually need. Difficult, I know, but give it a go and you will save money and heartache.

You're not potty to garden on clay

Although clay soils are often seen as being problematical – soggy and wet in winter and like concrete in summer – a good clay soil is one of the best soils you can have, as it will grow just about any plant well. Nutrients are held in a readily available way within clays, making these moist soils potentially very fertile. Although seedbeds are tricky, trees, shrubs and perennials usually grow very well once their roots penetrate the surrounding soil. These are easier to plant and care for, and grow fast on fertile clay soils. I know it is difficult, but try not to feel depressed by clay soil. It can prove to be the most fertile of soils and benefits from the ability to retain nutrients and water. It should be dug in winter with the clods left exposed to the elements which will help you break the soil down into more manageable bits. Then dig in lots of organic matter such as garden compost, leafmold and well rotted manure. It is hard work but then you are a gardener so stop moaning!

The crumb structure of clay soil can be improved by applying lime. If you don't want to raise the alkalinity of soil then use gypsum instead. Don't work the soil or walk on it when it is wet or sticky otherwise most of it will end up on your boots and you will just compact it further. Realistically it can take several seasons to create a better growing medium from a clay soil but the results will be worth the effort. Choosing plants that thrive in, or at least tolerate, heavy clay is a sensible starting point and always delay planting until spring. This will reduce the damaging effects of cold, wet soil which can cause fragile new roots to rot. The plant list opposite should give you some hope!

Steve's choice plants for a head start on clay

If you garden on clay and you are reading this book you must be a dedicated gardener 'cus it ain't easy! The following plants will tolerate the heavy conditions afforded by clay soil so at least you will have something to smile at whilst you make it workable for other less tolerant species ...

- *Cornus alba* (Dogwood)
- *Cotoneaster*
- *Crataegus laevigata* 'Paul's Scarlet' (Midland hawthorn)
- *Gunnera manicata* (Giant gunnera)
- *Hemerocallis* (Day lilly)
- *Hosta*
- *Ligularia* 'The Rocket' (Golden groundsel)
- *Persicaria campanulata* (Lesser knotweed)
- *Pulmonaria longifolia* (Lungwort)
- *Pyracantha* (Firethorn)
- *Rodgersia aesculifolia*
- *Salix matsudana tortuosa* (Corkscrew willow)
- *Solidago* (Golden rod)
- *Syringa vulgaris* (Common lilac)
- *Viburnum opulus* (Guelder rose)
- *Vitis coignetiae* (Crimson glory vine)
- *Weigela florida foliis purpureis*
- *Weigela* 'Florida Variegata'

Steve's choice plants for sandy soils

Although well-draining and aerated, sandy soils can often end up thirsty and hungry. The natural habitats of the following plants have these prevailing conditions so they will shrug them off in your garden ...

- *Acacia dealbata* (Mimosa tree)
- *Artemisia pontica* (Roman wormwood)
- *Ballota pseudodictamnus* (False dittiny)
- *Berberis darwinii* (Barberry)
- *Brachycome iberidifolia* (Swan River daisy)
- *Ceratostigma willmotianum* (Chinese plumbago)
- *Cercis siliquastrum* (Judas tree)
- *Cistus* species
- *Convolvulus cneorum* (Silverbush)
- *Corylus avellana 'Contorta'* (Corkscrew hazel)
- *Crambe cordifolia*
- *Dictamnus albus* (Burning bush)
- *Hibiscus syriacus* (Tree hollyhock)
- *Lavatera* 'Kew Rose' (Shrubby mallow)
- *Lavendula* (Lavender)
- *Papaver orientale* (Oriental poppy)
- *Portulaca grandiflora* (Moss rose)
- *Rosmarinus officinalis* (Rosemary)
- *Salvia officinalis tricolor* (Variegated sage)
- *Yucca gloriosa* (Spanish dagger)

A sandy soil can be draining

Sandy soils are well aerated, easy to cultivate, gritty to the touch and very free draining. They warm up quickly in spring giving plants a quicker start into growth. There is a price to pay for this advantage, however, as they are both thirsty and hungry because they dry out rapidly and might lack nutrients, which are easily washed through the soil in wet weather. Sandy soils therefore require more regular watering and feeding than other soils. In gardening, there is no such thing as a free lunch!

Sandy soil can be improved by adding plenty of nutrient-rich organic matter to both improve its water-holding capacity and provide more readily-available food. Additional plant food can be given in the form of balanced, slow release fertiliser granules. Mulching the soil surface to help reduce water evaporation and to avoid extreme fluctuations in surface temperature which could harm plant roots is also really beneficial. Plants that thrive on sandy soils are often accustomed to low nutrients and drought in their natural habitat. A useful list of such plants can be found on the opposite page.

A vegetable garden in sand needs a serious amount of work to give it the necessary amount of organic matter. Your best compost should be reserved for the vegetable garden, the finer and more mature the better. Once you think there is enough organic matter in the soil, then it can be topped up with soil conditioners and deluxe organic fertilisers. These include worm castings, blood and bone and pigeon manure. If you have chickens it is a good idea to rotate them with your vegetable crops. The chickens convert the crop waste into manure and they will even dig it in for you.

The bitter sweet battle for an acid soil

Acid loving plants originate from woodland areas and generally prefer cool, shady environments. The soil in these habitats is usually leafy, humus rich, moist but well drained. Mimicking these conditions will suit the huge range of plants that are likely to thrive on acid soils. There are, however, many acid loving plants that need and will tolerate sunny open sites so check carefully when buying and don't make assumptions. If the soil is excessively acid then it might fail to support even the most dedicated acid lovers and careful applications of lime will be required to moderate the acidity. Listed opposite are some suitable plants for acid soils.

If you want to grow acid loving plants (like azaleas and rhododendrons) but your soil is alkaline, the best solution is to create a raised bed filled with ericaceous compost on perforated polythene or grow the plants in containers. An annual top dressing with more ericaceous compost or peat will help and it is important to test the pH of your soil regularly. Lowering the acidity of lime rich soil is difficult, but flowers of sulphur can be applied or chelated iron compounds can be used. This will to help prevent chlorosis (the yellowing of leaves) which is a common problem of acid-loving, lime-hating, plants.

Steve's choice plants for acid soils

Providing that the soil is not excessively acid there is a huge range of plants that will thrive on an acid soil. Here are a few choice ones …

- *Acer palmatum*
- *Amelanchier lamarckii* (Snowy mespilus)
- *Callicarpa bodinieri var. giraldii Profusion* (Beauty berry)
- *Calluna, Daboecia* and *Erica* species (Heathers)
- *Camellia* varieties
- *Enkianthus campanulatus*
- *Fothergilla major*
- *Gaultheria*
- *Gentiana sino-ornata* (Gentian)
- *Iris sibirica* (Siberian iris)
- *Kalmia angustifolia* (Sheep laurel)
- *Leucothoe scarletta* (Switch ivy)
- *Magnolia solangeana* (tolerates acid soils)
- *Meconopsis betonicifolia* (Himalayan blue poppy)
- *Osmunda regalis* (Regal fern)
- *Erica* species (N.B. *Erica carnea* varieties will grow in alkaline soil)
- *Pieris formosa* (Himalayan pieris)
- *Rhododendron* varieties
- *Skimmia japonica* 'Rubella'

Steve's choice plants for chalk & limestone soils

The inventory of plants that will grow happily on chalk or limestone soils is endless. I got a bit carried away with this list which just shows you how these types of soil prevail across the globe ...

- *Arbutus unedo* (Strawberry tree)
- *Berberis darwinii* (Barberry)
- *Buddleia lindleyana* (Chinese butterfly bush)
- *Ceanothus* 'Autumnal Blue' (Californian lilac)
- *Clematis montana*
- *Cornus mas* (Cornelian cherry)
- *Cotinus coggygria* (Smoke bush)
- *Deutzia crenata* 'Nikko'
- *Dicentra spectabilis* (Bleeding heart)
- *Doronicum excelsum* (Leopard's bane)
- *Erysimum varieties* (Wallflower)
- *Gypsophila paniculata* (Baby's breath)
- *Kolkwitzia amabilis* (Beauty bush)
- *Philadelphus microphyllus* (Mock orange)
- *Potentilla fruticosa* (Shrubby cinquefoil)
- *Prunus* (Flowering cherries)
- *Rudbeckia* 'Goldquelle'
- *Syringa vulgaris* (Common lilac)
- *Verbascum* 'Gainsborough' (Mullein)
- *Veronica spicata* (Spiked speedwell)

Chalking up a result on limestone

Many of the world's favourite plants grow naturally on chalk and limestone. Apart from being alkaline, these soils can be rich and fertile as well as being well drained. Alkaline chalky soil with a pH of 7.5 or more is usually very shallow and stony, overlying chalk or limestone bedrock. A soil testing kit will instantly indicate whether your soil is acidic or alkaline. Water quality and soil type are closely linked, therefore, if you live in a hard water area, with high levels of lime deposits, it's likely your soil will be more alkaline. Growing on this type of soil does exclude a small proportion of plants, such as the acid-loving rhododendrons, pieris, skimmias and camellias, but you are still left with a huge range of plants to choose from. See my list opposite for a good selection.

Shallow soil over chalk can drain quickly. This can invariably lead to very hot and dry conditions in summer. Mulching and the addition of large amounts of compost will help to combat this. After several seasons of growth, some plants can show chlorosis (the yellowing of the leaves). This is due to iron and other vital nutrients becoming locked up by the soil's alkaline chemistry. A simple remedy is to apply sequestered iron annually as new growth starts in spring as well as regular applications of cold, black tea or broken tea bags – both rich in iron.

The windy city

Some of the most difficult conditions are found in gardens that suffer from extreme exposure. Planting shrubs around the perimeter of the garden to make effective, sheltering windbreaks for other plants is the secret to success. This makes the range of plants that can be grown within the garden so much greater and the choice of plants when the shelter is established is actually about the same as in a more naturally sheltered garden.

If you do have an exposed garden your first priority should be to lessen the full force of the wind chill, which can be the most damaging factor. This can initially be achieved by installing artificial windbreaks and by erecting individual protection measures, such as plastic tree shelters around each plant. Once the windbreak plants have become established the artificial shelters can be removed.

Exposed gardens can either be windy and cold, or suffer from extreme heat. They can suffer from deep frost or lie on a shallow wet soil. Where such conditions occur, most wild flowers will grow at their best. Where conditions are tough and few plants can survive, wild flowers will flower better. In such conditions, wild flowers have plenty of room for growth without much competition.

A useful list of plants for exposed sites can be found opposite.

Steve's choice plants for exposed sites

Exposed, windy conditions can spell death to many plants. The following plants are real tough nuts and can tolerate these extreme conditions, so make great perimeter windbreaks ...

- *Alnus incana* (Grey alder)
- *Anaphalis margaritacea* (Pearly everlasting)
- *Astrantia* 'Hadspen Blood' (Masterwort)
- *Berberis stenophylla* (Barberry)
- *Bergenia* (Elephant's ear)
- *Brunnera macrophylla* (Perennial forget-me-not)
- *Centaurea montana 'Alba'* (Perennial cornflower)
- *Crataegus monogyna* (Common hawthorn)
- *Euphorbia polychroma* (Spurge)
- *Ilex aquifolium* (Common holly)
- *Larix decidua* (European larch)
- *Prunus laurocerasus* (Cherry laurel)
- *Pyracantha coccinea* (Firethorn)
- *Salix alba* (White willow)
- *Sambucus niger* (Elderberry)
- *Spiraea nipponica*
- *Viburnum rhytidophyllum*
- *Viburnum tinus* (Laurustinus)

Steve's choice plants for a bog garden

The following plants will thrive in this moisture-rich environment and will provide interest for you and vital habitats for beneficial wildlife.

- *Alnus cordata* (Italian alder)
- *Aronia arbutifolia* (Red chokeberry)
- *Astilbe* varieties
- *Carex pendula* (Pendulous sedge)
- *Cimicifuga racemosa* (Black cohosh)
- *Cornus alba* 'Elegantissima' (Variegated dogwood)
- *Filipendula camtschatica* (Giant meadowsweet)
- *Gunnera manicata* (Giant gunnera)
- *Hosta* 'Big Daddy' (Plantain lily)
- *Ligularia dentata* 'Desdemona' (Golden groundsel)
- *Lysichiton americanus* (Skunk cabbage)
- *Metasequoia glyptostroboides* (Dawn redwood)
- *Oenanthe javanica* 'Flamingo' (Water dropwort)
- *Osmunda claytoniana* (Interrupted fern)
- *Primula prolifera* (Candelabra primula)
- *Rheum palmatum* (Chinese rhubarb)
- *Rodgersia aesculifolia* (Fingerleaf rodgersia)
- *Sagittaria latifolia* (Duck potato)
- *Salix alba vitellina* (Golden willow)
- *Zantedeschia aethiopica* (Arum lily)

Moisture-lovers

A bog garden is usually an area of moist soil in a low lying hollow or near a pond overflow. Plants that will grow in these areas are called moisture-lovers or bog plants but will not tolerate totally water logged soils. Boggy soil saturated with water is best planted with marginal aquatic plants.

A pond makes a superb focal point in the garden. It gives you the chance to grow a range of plants that you might never otherwise see and it helps to bring valuable wildlife into the garden. The plant list on page 41 gives a good selection of plants for any pond.

To get a balanced healthy pond you need to plant at different levels including floating or bottom-rooting oxygenating plants, with some hiding places for fish and other pond life. It is an advantage to the balance of the pond to have some moving water. This could be a fountain, a water fall or other type of water flow connected to a filtration system. The submerged plants help in removing excess nutrients from the water which might otherwise turn the water green and fuel the growth of algae. If you are having trouble with green algae in a pond then the barley straw tip on page 70 should help ...

Quick tip

THE BIG CHILL

If you pond freezes over in winter make holes in the ice using a saucepan full of hot water to remove toxic gases. Do not break the ice as the vibrations created could cause harm to fish or other wildlife under the ice.

Climbing the north-east face

North and east facing walls can be dry places since they often have a rain shadow at their base. It is best to plant in moisture retaining soil about 18" (46cm) away from the wall especially if over hung by the eaves of a house where rainfall is unable to penetrate.

East walls receive sun first thing in the morning and this can cause considerable damage to frozen leaves, buds, and flowers as the suns rays quickly thaw out growth, making them rupture and turn black. On a north wall the temperature rises slowly so is much less likely to cause damage to frozen growth, it is wise to take account of these facts when selecting plants and only plant the more hardy or latter developing types on the east wall.

The plants listed opposite are all tried and tested in these difficult positions so will give you great rewards, even in the face of seeming adversity. Some plants just love it tough!

Quick tip

MULCH ADO ABOUT NOTHING
Mulching around the base of any plants growing up or against a north or east facing wall with bark chippings or leaf mold can make all the difference to the performance of the plants. The mulch will do an excellent job of conserving moisture and also of warming up the soil which the sun rarely reaches. This will ensure earlier growth in spring.

Steve's choice plants for north & east facing walls

The following plants will perform really well on these testing aspects. Give them a go and you'll be pleasantly surprised!

- *Akebia quinata* (Chocolate vine)
- Camellia species
- *Chaenomeles speciosa* (Flowering quince)
- *Clematis montana*
- *Clematis* 'Nelly Moser'
- *Cotoneaster horizontalis*
- *Crinodendron hookerianum* (Chile lantern tree)
- *Forsythia suspensa* (Weeping forsythia)
- *Garrya elliptica* (Silk tassel bush)
- *Hedera colchica* 'Sulphur Heart' (Persian ivy)
- *Hydrangea petiolaris* (Climbing hydrangea)
- *Jasminum humile revolutum* (Yellow jasmine)
- *Lonicera x brownii* 'Dropmore Scarlet' (Honeysuckle)
- *Lonicera japonica* 'Halliana' (Japanese honeysuckle)
- *Mahonia* 'Winter Sun' and 'Charity'
- *Parthenocissus henryana* (Variegated Virginia creeper)
- *Parthenocissus tricuspidata* (Boston ivy)
- *Pyracantha* 'Golden Charmer' (Firethorn)
- *Rosa* 'Mme Alfred Carriere' (Climbing rose)
- *Ribes laurifolium* (Winter currant)
- *Vitis amurensis* (Amur grape)

The south-west elevation

The perfect site for growing wall shrubs is undoubtedly a south-west facing wall or fence. Plants growing on such walls bask in the heat of warm sunny days and usually respond by producing a greater profusion of flowers. These sheltered sites also make an ideal spot for a patio or sitting area so by including fragrant plants on the wall a welcoming outside entertaining area is instantly created.

Walls act like storage heaters, absorbing the day's heat and releasing it during the night and early morning. In colder parts of the country a warm wall can actually give several degrees of frost protection and thus make a real difference to the survival of slightly more tender climbers and wall plants plants. These walls do not receive early morning sun, so the plants growing on them warm up slowly after frost. This avoids the damage that rapid thawing can cause to frozen leaves and buds.

Plants may have to contend with drought in such a sheltered situation so, before planting, improve the soil with compost and plant 18" (46cm) away from the wall. Mulching to reduce surface evaporation (gravel or pebbles would be most suitable) is also a good idea.

The choice of climbers or wall plants that will flourish on a south-west facing wall or fence is truly endless. I have listed my favourites on pages 124 & 125 but I am sure that you will discover other gems that will suit your particular garden if you are lucky enough to have this prized aspect available.

Shady & thirsty

The combination of shade and drought presents the gardener with a real challenge. Few plants are able to tolerate a situation where both light and moisture are lacking. The coping measure is to improve the soil with lots of organic matter.

Plant chosen species a lot closer than is usually recommended, mulch well after planting and consider establishing an under planting carpet of drought-resistant ground cover plants like Pachysandra or Tellima. All these actions help to retain moisture and reduce surface evaporation. Shrubby plants will grow more slowly than usual and generally plantings will take longer to establish. The reduced vigour, however, will mean there should not be as much of a need to prune. The plant list on pages 102-103 should give you some useful ideas.

Hot & thirsty

For any plant that is not adapted to cope, a hot, dry spot in the garden can prove difficult. Such sites present a challenge to plant survival because of the lack of moisture and the scorching effect of the very hot sun.

Plants, such as those listed on page 63, will thrive in these conditions because they have characteristics which are both beautiful and practical. Grey, silver and blue leaved plants; those that are clothed in fine hair or those that have a waxy surface will all deflect the burning rays of the sun. Plants with fragrant foliage often exude volatile oils which act as a sun block and low growing succulent plants with thick, fleshy leaves have the ability to store water.

Steve's choice plants for south & west facing walls & fences

The choice of plants for these wonderfully sunny aspects is vast. The following are some of my favourites but I could have gone on and on and on …

- *Abelia schumannii*
- *Abeliophyllum distichum* (White forsythia)
- *Abutilon* 'Souvenir de Bonn'
- *Acacia baileyana purpurea* (Cootamundra wattle)
- *Actinidia kolomikta* (Kiwi)
- *Ampelopsis brevipedunculata* (Porcelain vine)
- *Buddleia crispa* (Butterfly bush)
- *Callistemon citrinus* (Bottlebrush)
- *Carpenteria californica* (Bush anemone)
- *Ceanothus* species
- *Chaenomeles* speciosa (Ornamental quince)
- *Chimonanthus praecox* (Fragrant wintersweet)
- *Clematis* 'Dr Ruppel'
- *Clematis* 'Jakmannii'
- *Clematis armandii* 'Apple Blossom'
- *Clematis cirrhosa balearica* 'Freckles'
- *Cytisus battandieri* (Pineapple broom)
- *Daphne odora* (Winter daphne)
- *Desmodium elegans var. spicatum*
- *Erythrina crista-galli* (Coral tree)

- *Feijoa sellowiana* (Pineapple guava)
- *Fremontodendron* 'California Glory'
- *Itea ilicifolia*
- *Jasminum beesianum* (Red jasmine)
- *Jasminum officinale* 'Argenteovariegatum' (Variegated summer jasmine)
- *Lonicera periclymenum* 'Sweet Sue' (Honeysuckle)
- *Lonicera x americana* (Honeysuckle)
- *Magnolia grandiflora*
- *Myrtus communis* 'Variegata' (Variegated sweet myrtle)
- *Olea europaea* (Olive tree)
- *Passiflora caerulea* 'Constant Elliot' (Passion flower)
- *Philadelphus burkwoodii* (Mock orange)
- *Piptanthus nepalensis* (Evergreen laburnum)
- *Robinia hispida* (Rose acacia)
- *Rosa* 'Madame Grégoire Staechelin' (Climbing rose)
- *Rosa x odorata* 'Mutabilis' (Vigorous shrub rose)
- *Rosa* 'Shropshire Lad' (Climbing rose)
- *Solanum jasminoides* 'Album' (Potato vine)
- *Trachelospermum jasminoides* (Star jasmine)
- *Vitis vinifera* 'Purpurea' (Claret grape vine)
- *Weigela florida* 'Aureovariegata'
- *Wisteria sinensis*

There can be no
other occupation like
gardening in which,
if you were to creep up
behind someone at their
work, you would find
them smiling.

Mirabel Osler

Odds & sods

chapter 5
Odds & sods

A tight spot for your onions

Storing onions over the winter can be a mouldy experience if they touch each other. A good circulation of air around the bulbs is needed and this can be easily achieved by storing the onions in old tights or stockings. Just drop an onion in and tie the material above it into a knot then put another onion in, tie a knot and so on and so forth. When you need an onion simply cut the lowest one off just below the knot. This same trick works for storing garlic bulbs with the added benefit of a vampire-free existence!

High fat, homemade feeder

Feeding the birds is a very rewarding hobby and, in order to get those that don't migrate to stay in your garden all year, you must switch the food in autumn to one with a high fat content. This will help the birds build up a good layer of special fatty tissue (called adipose tissue) to survive the winter. Making your own high fat feeder is easy, fun, and the birds will love it! Melt 8oz of lard in a pan and mix in a tablespoon each of porridge oats, wild birdseed, chopped peanuts and dried fruit. Before the mixture sets pour into empty yoghurt pots whist holding a length of string dangling in the middle of each pot. Leave the pots in the fridge to set then simply tip out your bird's banquet and hang outside by the string from a tree or on the bird table.

Rock of ages

Newly acquired rocks added to an existing rockery, or new bricks used to repair an old wall can stick out like a sore thumb until they have weathered for a year or so. You can easily speed up this aging process with nothing more than a pot of natural 'live' yoghurt and a roll of cling film, which is best done when the weather is warm. Paint the rock or brick surface with a generous layer of the yoghurt, which must be 'live' as this contains the mix of bacteria that holds the key to this tip working. Next completely cover the yoghurt painted surface with cling film and just wait.

After about two weeks remove the cling film and wash off any remaining yoghurt. Amazingly the rest will have become home to different types of algae and maybe even some lichen. The whole rock will also have a dark, weathered look, as though it had been there in your garden for years.

Quick tip

PASTRY BIRD FEEDERS – A REAL TWEET!
Don't throw away any pastry off cuts when baking. Mould them into different fun shapes (the kids will love to help!), press birdseed into the surface and make a hole for hanging before baking in the oven. The result is a selection of stylish and fun bird feeders to hang around the garden.

Temper, temper!

A golden rule of gardening – never prune in a bad mood! Pruning is one of those tasks for which you need to feel relaxed and at one with yourself and the plants around you, letting the kind, gentle hand of Mother Nature guide your every cut with exquisite perfection. If you're in a strop you'll just chop the lot down! Post-spousal-argument gardening is best kept to heavy digging or wood-chopping.

The oil & water trick

Mowing the lawn when the grass is a bit damp can be a nightmare and cleaning the mower can take longer than the initial task. Avoid wet grass sticking to the blades and underside of the mower by lightly spraying the areas with a little sunflower oil before you mow. Amazingly the wet grass will not stick. Oil and water, you see, do not mix and the damp grass cannot stick so it just drops off. Be sure to remove the oil with WD-40 before you cut dry grass or the opposite will happen.

Berry bonanza

When picking blackberries, raspberries etc, having two hands free means more berries picked in the time you have. A large empty plastic milk container or 2 litre plastic pop bottle, bottom cut off, turned upside down and held round your waist with a belt through the handle makes a brilliant berry collector! The look of envy from other collectors on the hedge is worth the bit of effort you have gone to. A large bucket at your feet should be available into which you can decant your spoils.

Building supplies for the birds

Finding good nesting material can be a real headache for birds in late winter and early spring. You can help them by filling a net bag such as an orange or Brussels sprout net with all manner of useful nest building materials and hanging outside so that the birds can easily pull bits through the net and use it like haberdashery. Materials that birds find really useful include straw, shredded paper, strands of wool & cotton, animal or human hair & thin twigs. One of the best things I have found, which House Martins in particular seem to like, is Shredded Wheat breakfast cereal! The birds don't eat it – they wet it with saliva and use it as a mortar for 'plastering' their nests to give them a modern 'oatmeal' look. It could catch on! Along with all this construction assistance, feed the birds regularly and they will become frequent visitors to your garden.

Fading flowers

If you have ever wondered why your vases of beautiful cut flowers don't last more than a few days, take a look around the room. If you have a bowl of fruit anywhere – that is probably the reason. The gas (ethylene), which fruits give off as they ripen, will fade cut flowers very quickly. Bananas are the worst culprits and will see off a whole vase of flowers single-handedly overnight! The further the distance the fruit is away from the flowers the longer the blooms will last.

Longer lasting fence posts

A fence post will last a lot longer in the ground before it rots if you soak the bottom 18" (46cm) in old engine oil for a few days then wrap the end in cling film before concreting in the ground. A bit of effort, but you have added years to the life of the post.

Nature's own bird feeder

When you pick up a large pinecone with the open bracts that have released all their seeds, what you unknowingly have in your hands is Mother Nature's custom made bird feeder. The bracts are springy and will hold all kinds of tasty treats for the birds – nuts, fat, bread, cheese, stale cake or biscuits, bacon rind, boiled potato – whatever suitable scraps you can find. Once filled, you can easily hang it up with string tied around the top bracts or through a hole drilled in the top. At Christmastime, before filling with food, spray the cones with gold or silver paint for a really festive look. Kids can easily make these and fill them with different nuts, wrap in cellophane and give as unique gifts.

Quick tip

SORT OUT YOUR LOOSE ENDS

An old jam jar with a hole punched through the lid makes a great storage container for those unravelled balls of garden twine or string. Put the ball into the jar and poke the free end of the twine through the hole in the lid. Replace the lid and you have a clever little string dispenser.

Bug-free wellies

It's happened to every gardener at some time – you pull on your wellies only to feel the telltale wriggle of that huge spider that has taken up residence in the toe end or the slimy crunch of an over-wintering snail. Avoid this nightmare by simply treating yourself to a brand new pair of tights. Immediately after taking off your Wellingtons, cover each one with one leg of the tights. Now nothing can crawl inside overnight.

Flat lemonade puts the fizz into cut flowers

Forget the fancy food you can buy to mix with water to keep your cut flowers fresh in the vase. Flat lemonade does the trick just as well Make sure the lemonade is completely flat, as carbonated drink can have a detrimental effect with the gas potentially causing blockages in some flower stems. The sugars and other minerals in the flat lemonade help keep the blooms looking good for days. The cheap, own brand lemonade from supermarkets is the most cost effective way of feeding your cut flowers as you probably wouldn't want to drink it anyway.

A green tomato hand cleaner

The green stains that are inevitably left on your hands after removing the side shoots of your tomato plants can be really difficult to remove. Here's the easy way... before washing your stained hands with soap, cut a green tomato in half and rub the cut side vigorously over the stains. The stains are then easily removed because the acid from the green tomato un-fixes the green dye on your skin. The same plant that caused the problem has helped you solve it!

Steve's top plants for an autumn leaf display

If you want to really set the sparks flying in the autumn garden, don't just think flowers – think leaves as well. You will not be disappointed by any of the following …

- *Acer palmatum* 'Senkaki'
- *Acer palmatum* 'Osakazuki'
- *Aronia arbutifolia* 'Erecta' (Chokeberry)
- *Amelanchier lamarkii* (Snowy Mespilus)
- *Berberis x media* 'Red Jewel' (Barberry)
- *Callicarpa japonica* (Beauty Berry)
- *Cornus alba* 'Kesselringii' (Red-barked dogwood)
- *Cornus alba* 'Sibirica' (another Red-barked dogwood!)
- *Cornus sanguinea* 'Winter Flame' (Common dogwood)
- *Cotinus* 'Flame' (Smoke bush)
- *Euonymus europaeus* 'Red Cascade' (Spindleberry)
- *Fothergilla gardenia* (needs acid soil)
- *Hamamelis x intermedia* 'Feuerzauber'
- *Hydrangea quercifolia* (Oak-leaved hydrangea – great in a tub)
- *Oxydendrum arboreum* (Sorrel tree - needs acid soil)
- *Parthenocissus tricuspidata* (Boston ivy)
- *Prunus incisa* 'Kojo-no-mai' (Fuji cherry)
- *Ribes odoratum* (Buffalo currant)
- *Spirea betulifolia var. amiliana*
- *Vaccinium corymbosum* (Highbush blueberry)

Gardening diary

How often do you begin a new gardening year with the memories of the successes and failures of the previous year fading fast? It is so easy to forget important details that made a difference when they occurred months before. Recording all your gardening achievements and cock-ups with a camera and a diary makes next year's planning so much easier. Do this throughout the season and be sure to make a note of sowing times, weather conditions etc ... You can then review everything on a cold January evening — recalling the joys of the previous summer and getting excited about the prospects of the year to come. Your picture diaries will become a great source of reference, interest (and probably amusement) in the years that follow.

Garden with soap for that manicured look

If you are one of those gardeners who prefers not to wear gloves when gardening, then you will relate to this problem: the 'grubby nail' scenario. After a day in the garden you will spend an eternity scrubbing to remove the soil imbedded deep under your nails, in preparation for that special night out. Use this tip for crystal clear nails every time. Before you go out into the garden in the first place run your nails firmly over the surface of a bar of soap and fill them with tiny bits of it. When you come to wash your hands later the soap from under your nails can be easily removed and not one speck of dirt will remain!

"Cultivate a garden for the nose, and the eyes will take care of themselves."

Robert Louis Stevenson

Steve's favourite 'winter-wonder' flowering trees and shrubs

Winter is often forgotten as a time for injecting flower-power into the garden. These beauties come into their own when most other plants have shut up shop ...

- *Chaenomeles speciosa* (Ornamental quince)
- *Chimonanthus praecox* (Wintersweet)
- *Cornus mas* (Cornelian cherry)
- *Corylopsis* (Fragrant winterhazel)
- *Corylus avellana* 'Contorta' (Corkscrew hazel)
- *Daphnae bholua* 'Jaqueline Postill'
- *Erica carnea* 'Pink Spangles' (Winter flowering heather)
- *Garrya elliptica* (Silk tassel bush)
- *Hamamelis x intermedia* 'Jelena' (Witch hazel)
- *Hamamelis mollis* (Chinese witch hazel)
- *Jasminum nudiflorum* (Winter jasmine)
- *Lonicera fragrantissima* (Honeysuckle)
- *Lonicera purpusii* 'Winter Beauty' (Honeysuckle)
- *Lonicera standishii* (Honeysuckle)
- *Mahonia* 'Charity'
- *Parrotia persica* (Persian ironwood)
- *Prunus x subhirtella* 'Autumnalis' (Rosebud cherry)
- *Rhododendron dauricum* 'Midwinter'
- *Viburnum x bodnantense* 'Dawn'
- *Viburnum farreri*

The garden cure for traveller's tummy

This is not exactly a gardening tip, more advice on a couple of useful plants to grow – lemon verbena and angelica. Sprigs of these two aromatic herbs make wonderful cures for travel sickness. Place them under the feet of the susceptible car passenger and tell them to periodically tread on them. This action will release the aroma, which will quickly alleviate nausea as well as making the car smell fresh.

Impressive autumn masterpiece

Autumn can be one of the most beautiful times of the year in the garden. Taking photos of the wonderful leaf colours sometimes just doesn't capture the true beauty. Don't let nature's annual firework display go to waste so collect nice examples of colourful autumn leaves and press them between some heavy books for a few weeks. Then buy a cheap clip-glass picture frame and arrange the leaves in an overlapping design on the backboard. Clip the glass back on and voilá, you have an inexpensive and individual masterpiece.

Quick tip

MAKE A NOTE OF THIS TIP
Always get into the habit of taking a small notebook and pencil whenever you go into your own garden or to visit other gardens. You can then easily jot down all the must-have plants you discover and planting ideas that come to mind. It's amazing how much you forget when you get back home.

Don't get in a flap over floppy tulips

It has happened to everyone I am sure. A vase of tulips looks wonderful for a few hours then the heads start to droop. Don't despair because help is at hand from an unusual source – the humble dressmaker's pin. All that is required is for you to carefully push a pin in and out, right through the stem of the tulip, just at the bottom of the floppy bit. Then wait. After half an hour or so the tulip head should rise up again!

Before you apply to join The Magic Circle let me explain the secret of the 'trick'. When you fill a vase with water from the tap you are dragging bubbles of air into the water. Most plant stems have a similar diameter all the way up but tulip stems are a bit different. The hollow stem actually narrows slightly near the flower head and air bubbles present in the water of the vase get trapped in this narrow part, preventing water from reaching the bloom and hence resulting in a droop. Using the pin simply releases the trapped air and the flower head can drink again.

To avoid this happening, get into the habit of filling a vase with water and then leaving it to stand for an hour or so before putting in the flowers. This time will allow the air bubbles to dissipate out of the water.

Rank chrysanths

If you have a bunch of chrysanthemums in a vase of water you just know what will happen. Within a few days the water will become cloudy and will smell rank. This is caused by a quick build up of bacteria in the water and it only seems to happen with chrysanthemums. More frequent water changing is called for but who, in their busy life, can remember to do this? Well, worry not as all you need to do is bleach and go! Literally a few drops of household bleach put into the vase before adding the water will prevent the nasty bacteria from taking a hold and you will never have the problem again.

Potty presents

Original gifts can be made by buying a range of cheap terracotta pots, various colours of acrylic paint and some clear external varnish. Paint designs on the pots and varnish when dry for frost protection. You can then give one of your unique pots as a present on its own or buy a complementary coloured flowering plant to sit in it. If you know your gift-recipient well then you could be really clever and paint a small pot to match the décor of their conservatory or lounge and include a foliage plant for style. This pot-art idea is also an ideal way for young children to produce a novel gift for grandma that she will cherish for ever.

"A perfect summer day is when the sun is shining, the breeze is blowing, the birds are singing, and the lawn mower is broken. "

Anon

Steve's top beautiful berrying shrubs

If you just grow plants for their flowers then you might be missing a trick. Often, if you just wait a while after the flowers have gone, you (and the birds!) could be rewarded with a real feast of gorgeous berries …

- *Ampelopsis brevipendunculata*
- *Berberis darwinii* (Barberry)
- *Callicarpa bodinieri var. giraldii* 'Profusion' (Beauty berry)
- *Clerodendrum bungei*
- *Cotoneaster frigidus* 'Cornubia'
- Crataegus monogyna (Common hawthorn)
- *Euonymus europaeus* 'Red Cascade' (Spindleberry)
- *Gaultheria mucronata* (Prickly heath)
- *Ilex aquifolium* (Holly)
- *Leycesteria formosa* (Pheasant berry)
- *Mahonia aquifolium* (Oregon grape)
- *Prunus laurocerastus* (Cherry laurel)
- *Pyracantha coccinea* 'Orange Glow' (Firethorn)
- *Rosa rugosa* (Hedgehog rose)
- *Sambucus nigra* (Elderberry)
- *Skimmia fortunei*
- *Symphoricarpos albus* (Snowberry)
- *Vaccinium ovatum* (Box blueberry)
- *Viburnum davidii*
- *Viburnum opulus* (Guelder rose)

Steve's calendar for a lovely lawn

March:

As soon as the grass begins to grow and the conditions are right, gently rake the lawn to remove leaves and surface rubbish. The first cut should be just to remove the top ½" (12mm) of the grass. Close cutting now will result in severe yellowing. If moss is a real problem, apply a liquid moss killer, and rake out the black, dead moss two weeks later.

April:

A busy month! Mow often enough to stop the grass growing too long, but do not cut lower than about 1½" (38mm). Don't mow if the grass is very wet or frosted. Always brush off any debris such as leaves, twigs and especially worm casts, with a besom broom if available. Feeding and weeding can begin towards the end of the month as long as the grass and the weeds are actively growing, so have a careful inspection. This is a good time for sowing a new lawn as grass seed germinates quicker with the changes in temperature that can occur in spring.

May:

Increase the frequency of mowing as necessary and lower the height of cut to about 1" (2.5cm). Usually weekly mowing can begin. If feeding and weeding was not carried out last month then do it as soon as possible before things get serious. Water the lawn if a prolonged dry spell occurs: don't wait for the grass to go yellow. Regularly check over the lawn for any signs of problems.

June:

Summer mowing should be underway by now, cutting twice a week if possible to keep the grass to about 1" (2.5cm). If a dry spell occurs then reduce mowing and raise the cutting height. Giving the lawn a light raking before mowing will help keep clover runners under control. This is the time for summer lawn feeding, using a high nitrogen product. Carefully examine the turf: if weeds are a problem then treat as described for April. If hot weather has baked the soil surface, then prick the lawn with a sharp fork before watering or feeding and weeding.

July:

Mow regularly at the summer height; water if the weather is dry; rake as for June; spot weed any persistent weeds that appear. If you are on holiday for a fortnight or more then make arrangements for mowing and watering in your absence, otherwise you could undo all your efforts of the past months.

August:

Same general treatment as for July. August is the last month for you to carry out any weed killing or feeding with a nitrogen-rich tonic. If you return from holiday to long grass then raise the cutting height on the mower for the first cut. If you return from holiday to dead grass then keep the bottle of Ouzo you bought to thank your neighbour for looking after your lawn, and drink it yourself. Happy mowing!

September:

Another busy month for the lawn! Increase the interval between mowing and raise the cutting height to 1½" (38mm). This allows the grass to grow a little higher, and will help to reduce the chance of frost penetrating the turf and damaging it. Get rid of the moss first, using a moss killer. Two weeks later you can scarify the lawn to remove the dead moss. Moss is often a sign of poor growing conditions, such as bad drainage, excessive shade, compaction, low fertility and over-acidity. To tackle poor drainage and compaction, aerate the lawn and apply a top dressing (see October). To improve fertility, feed the lawn. To remove shade, prune back overhanging trees and shrubs. To reduce acidity, apply lime – such as ground chalk or ground limestone – at no more than 1.5oz per sq yd.

Perk up a tired lawn this month by giving it a feed. Use an autumn lawn fertiliser, as this will be high in phosphates and potash and low in nitrogen encouraging strong roots to develop but not top growth. Many autumn lawn treatments contain ingredients that will actively control cast-forming worms and prevent some of the common diseases. Never be tempted to use spring lawn fertilisers because they contain high levels of nitrogen. This encourages soft, sappy leaf growth, which is vulnerable to disease. September is a good month for lawn repairs with turf or seed, as the soil is warm and moist.

October:

Scarify the lawn this month. This means vigorously raking the lawn to remove the layer of old grass clippings, moss and other rubbish that builds up in the turf, encouraging disease. Getting rid of this will allow water and fertilisers to reach the grass roots more easily and in turn will improve grass growth. Scarifying also stimulates the grass to produce side shoots and runners. You can use a spring-tine rake, or hire or buy an electric scarifier. Improve the drainage on compacted areas of the lawn by aerating it with a garden fork or hollow-tine tool. Once you've aerated the soil, late October it is a good time to apply a top dressing. A simple mixture of three parts of loam, six parts of sharp sand and one part of peat substitute will suit most soils. Apply at about 4lb per sq yd and brush it into the lawn surface.

Regular mowing comes to an end during October. For the last cut or two raise the cutter height a fraction and make sure that you brush off any raindrops or dew before cutting. Rake up any fallen leaves.

November:
If we have an extended autumn you might wish to mow the grass with the blades set high. Clean all equipment and book the mower in for a winter service. Coat the blades with a little cooking oil to ensure they do not develop any rust.

December / January:
These months offer a slack time in what is usually a busy year of lawn care. Keep off the grass if it is frozen or very wet.

February:
Watch out for worm casts from worms, brush them off and await the appearance of a wonderful lawn in March.

"If you hoe when you don't need to hoe, you never need to hoe."

A Aslett

Choice plants for damp, shady sites

Damp shade is another problem area. In nature, we are likely to get damp shade in woodland where there is a combination of low light and potentially wet surfaces. If you are pondering over a damp, shady area then the following plants should work quite well.

- *Aconitum carmichaelii (Monkshood)*
- *Asplenium scolopendrium (Hart's tongue fern)*
- *Astilbe (False goat's beard)*
- *Brunnera macrophylla (Perennial forget-me-not)*
- *Clematis montana*
- *Convallaria majalis (Lily of the valley)*
- *Crocosmia 'Lucifer'*
- *Dicentra spectabilis (Bleeding heart)*
- *Fritillaria*
- *Glaucidium palmatum (Japanese wood poppy)*
- *Hydrangea serrata*
- *Iris pseudacorus*
- *Omphalodes cappadocica (Navelwort)*
- *Primula (esp Primula viallii)*
- *Ranunculus (esp. R. ficaria 'Brazen Hussy')*
- *Ruscus aculeatus (Buther's broom)*
- *Sisyrinchium striatum*
- *Trollius europaeus (Globeflower)*
- *Vinca major 'Variegata' (Greater periwinkle)*
- *Zantedeschia aethiopica (Hardy arum lily)*

Notes

Gone to
potting shed—
back in 5 x

Index of plant lists

General index

M

Magnesium
  deficiency, 29
Male urine, 59, 97
Mare's-tail, 38, 77
Margarine containers,
  28
Marigolds, French, 67
Mice, 34
Mildew, rose, 82
Milk, 82
Milk container, 131
Mineral felt, 81
Mint, 71
Mirrors, handbag, 89
Moles, 96
Mop head, cotton, 12
Moss, 144, 146
Moving shrubs, 34
Mowing, 131
Mulch, carpet, 39
Mulching, 84
Muscle spray, 68

N

Nail polish, 19
Nails, dirty, 136
Net bag, 132
Nettles, 53
North-facing aspect,
  120-121
Notebook, 137

O

Oasis, florist's, 30
Oil, engine, 19, 133

Oil, sunflower, 131
Onion sets, 81
Onions, storing, 129
Oranges, 99
Orchids, 14
Origins of plants, 103

P

Paraffin, 34
Pastry, 130
Pea seeds, 34
Perennials,
  supporting, 48
Petroleum jelly, 83
Pigeon droppings, 58
Pin, dressmaker's, 140
Pine cone, 133
Pine needles, 58
Plant labels, 19
Plant origins, 103
Plant ties, 12, 33, 48
Planting, 39
Planting, close, 101
Pollination, 40, 42
Pond algae, 72
Pond weed, 71
Pond plants, 41, 119
Pontica bucket, 19
Pop bottle, plastic, 21,
  29, 38, 89, 131
Pot painting, 141
Potassium, 57
Propagator tops,
  homemade, 17
Pruning, 131

R

Rabbit-proof
  perennials, 85
Rabbit-proof shrubs,
  80
Rabbit straw, 60
Ralgex, 68
Rocks, ageing, 130
Roll-on deodorant, 67
Roofing felt, 81
Rose mildew, 82
Roses, 57, 71, 84
Rubber band, 11
Rubber glove, 77

S

Salt, 76, 82
Sand, 12
Sandy soil, 111
Scented leaf plants,
  55
Sealant, silicone,
  36-37
Secateurs, 46
Seed drills, 48
Seed storage, 49
Seeds, collecting, 38
Seeds, sowing tiny, 26
Shady aspect, 102,
  103, 123
Sheep droppings, 58
Shower caps, 17
Shredded Wheat, 132
Shrubs, moving, 34

The Greatest Gardening Tips in the World – DVD

If you like this gardening tips book then you will love this! A fun and informative DVD full of great gardening tips and advice presented by award-winning TV & radio gardening presenter, Steve Brookes. Prepare to be amazed as Steve guides you around his garden showing a host of money-saving and innovative tips for growing healthier plants.

Experienced, novice and even reluctant gardeners will love this entertaining look at the challenges faced in every garden.

The Greatest Gardening Tips in the World – DVD is just £12.99. To buy copies of the DVD and additional copies of this great little book (£9.99), visit ***www.stevebrookes.com*** where you can buy, securely online and have your order delivered postage free in the UK. Postage charges apply to overseas orders including The Republic of Ireland.

Alternatively, you can order by post, making cheques payable to 'Steve Brookes' and sending your order to:

The Greatest Gardening Tips
60 Loxley Road
Stratford-upon-Avon
Warwickshire CV37 7DR

Tel: 01789 267124

For overseas orders by post, please contact us first for advice on the additional postage cost.